Innovative Worship

Vital
MINISTRY™
Loveland, Colorado

Innovative Worship

Copyright © 1999 Vital Ministry Books

Visit our Web site: **www.grouppublishing.com**

Credits

Contributing Authors: Karen Dockrey, Debbie Gowensmith, Mikal Keefer, Jan Kershner, Karl Leuthauser, Danny Martin, Kelly Martin, Erin McKay, Dennis McLaughlin, Kathy Jo Mitchell, Ken Niles, Lori Haynes Niles, Amy Simpson, Dave Thornton, and Helen Turnbull

Editor: Dennis R. McLaughlin
Creative Development Editor: Paul Woods
Chief Creative Officer: Joani Schultz
Copy Editor: Debbie Gowensmith
Art Director: Kari K. Monson
Cover Art Director: Jeff A. Storm
Cover Designer: Alan Furst Design
Computer Graphic Artist: Pat Miller
Cover Photographer: Brian Ross-Tanning
Illustrator: Christine Nuanez-Voegtle
Production Manager: Peggy Naylor

Library of Congress Cataloging-in-Publication Data

Innovative worship / [contributing authors, Karen Dockrey ... et al.].
      p. cm.
     Includes index.
     ISBN 0-7644-2097-6 (alk. paper)
     1. Worship programs. I. Dockrey, Karen, 1955-   .
  BV198.I56   1999
  264--dc21   99-21808
                                  CIP

10 9 8 7 6 5 4 3 2 1   08 07 06 05 04 03 02 01 00 99

Printed in the United States of America.

Contents

Holidays

Christmas

Easter

Introduction

Have you ever noticed that some things in life just don't seem to add up? For example, the Bible is filled with stories, lessons, and acts of worship that involve all five of the human senses, but when you visit many worship services today, the most you do is watch and listen. It just doesn't add up!

On many occasions, Jesus himself engaged those around him in lessons and acts of worship that involved all the senses. Just thumb through the Gospels, and you'll be reminded of meaningful experiences, including washing of feet, anointing with perfume, tasting of bread, and touching of a cloak.

And who can forget King David's joyful praise and public celebration in the city streets of Jerusalem? Yes, Michal his wife probably wasn't the only one who questioned David's spontaneous act of "leaping and dancing before the Lord" (2 Samuel 6:16). But at the very least, David demonstrated that worship can be active and need not always be quiet and passive.

Between Jesus' examples of creating experiences that engaged all the senses and David's demonstration of spontaneous, creative worship, we are definitely provided with a picture of worship that calls for active participation.

Yes, worship is a holy moment. It's a pure expression of love, honor, and praise for a supreme God. But the biblical picture includes joyful celebration, spontaneity, and creativity. If there is a solemn and subdued moment when the hand of God touches the heart of the worshipper, the journey into that moment need not be a somber affair.

What an opportunity! What a responsibility and challenge! Certainly worship that is active and dynamic calls for more than good preaching and good music. It calls for planning, congregational involvement, prayer, and definitely a touch of creativity.

The bad news is that planning for creative worship takes time. The good news is that Vital Ministry Books recognizes that time is one of the most valuable commodities in the lives of pastors. Thus we are committed to providing pastors with quality resources that will help take some of the "bite" out of the time it takes to plan creative worship.

We created *Innovative Worship* to assist you as you plan for meaningful worship. As you begin to incorporate some of these creative ideas into your services, you'll quickly notice that the worship experience is becoming more meaningful and memorable.

The activities in this book include creative calls to worship, building dedications, acts of praise, celebrations of the Lord's Supper, music experiences, offerings, creative readings, benedictions, invocations, prayers, pre-service greetings, sharing times, creative movements, meditations, and worship postures. We have tailored some of the activities for specific holidays. For quick reference, we've included both a Scripture index and an activity index.

If you've never before used active and interactive activities that involve all five senses in teaching, preaching, and worship, you'll quickly see that in no way do they detract from that solemn moment when the hand of God meets the heart of the worshipper. What you will discover is that these "worship sparks" make the journey into that moment much more meaningful and memorable.

So why wait? Incorporate one of the activities into your next worship experience, and just wait and see how quickly things begin to add up in a very positive way!

General Worship

The Wall of Jericho

Activity: Creative movement, building dedication

Scripture: Joshua 6:1-20

You'll need a Bible and a handout for each worshipper that includes seven prayer themes. Use the following suggested themes as a guide:

- Praise God for our congregation and this building.
- Dedicate our congregation and this building to God's service.
- Pray for the pastoral staff.
- Pray for the children's ministry.
- Pray for the youth ministry.
- Pray for ministry to families.
- Pray for the neighborhood around the church.
- Pray for revival in our congregation.
- Pray for the walls of racial discrimination to fall down.
- Pray for healing in relationships.
- Pray for physical healing of people in the congregation.

Overview

Joshua and the Israelites faithfully obeyed God's command to walk around the wall of Jericho seven days in a row. As a result of their obedience, the wall fell down and God gave them the city as promised.

- This prayer march will give your congregation members an opportunity to involve their whole bodies in prayer. This activity is particularly appropriate to dedicate a new building or to kick off a time of renewal or revival in your church.

Read aloud Joshua 6:1-5, 15-17. Say:

> **Today we are going to re-enact this great event by walking around the outside of the church building seven times. The object is for you to pray, using a different prayer theme with each trip around the building. The walk should be a time of quiet meditation and prayer. When you have finished, please gather back in the worship area.**

Give each worshipper a copy of the handout as he or she walks out of the sanctuary.

(Variation: Consider ending this activity with cheers, shouting, or the blasting of trumpets.)

Make Music to God

Activity: Call to worship

Scripture: Psalm 33:2-4

You'll need inexpensive, small, round bells sold in many sewing and craft stores and copies of the "Make Music to God" handout (p. 14) placed in worship programs.

Overview

The psalms encourage worshippers to enter into God's presence and create a new song that is pleasing to him.

• This activity provides a fun and musical way to praise God at the beginning of worship.

As worshippers arrive, provide small bells. Ask worshippers to follow the instructions in their worship programs as they are seated.

Colorful Praise

Activity: Act of praise

Scripture: 2 Samuel 6:1-5, 14-15; Psalm 9:1-2

You'll need markers and colorful balloons.

Overview

When the Lord helped Israel defeat the Philistines and bring the ark back to Jerusalem, King David and all of Israel celebrated "before the Lord" with songs, a parade, and dancing.

• This colorful activity uses balloons to encourage worshippers to openly give praise for the work God has done in their lives. It works especially well just prior to or after prayer.

Remind worshippers that when God works in our lives, it's cause for celebration and for sharing joy with others. Give a colorful balloon to each participant, and give one marker to each row for people to share. Have worshippers blow up the balloons,

Make Music to God

The bells were provided as a way to honor and praise God in preparation for today's worship service. Rather than visiting with one another this morning, begin ringing your bells. Although you don't need to ring the bells constantly, the congregation as a whole is encouraged to fill in any gaps with the music of the bells. To begin worship, the worship leader will ask you to read in unison the following verses from Psalm 33. Continue ringing your bells until we've finished reading these verses together.

"Praise the Lord with the harp; make music to him on the ten-stringed lyre. Sing to him a new song; play skillfully, and shout for joy. For the word of the Lord is right and true; he is faithful in all he does" (Psalm 33:2-4).

think about something wonderful God has done in their lives, and write it on their balloons. Be sure people understand that other people will read their balloons.

To visualize God's work in their lives and to praise God for what he's doing, have worshippers bop their balloons in the air for a minute of colorful and fun praise. Encourage worshippers to see each balloon as a new, wondrous reason to praise God. As the balloons are flying around, invite participants to sing a well-known praise song.

After a minute of balloon fun, have worshippers each grab a balloon close to them and read what it says. Encourage people to take the balloons home and continue to thank God for his work in their own lives and in the lives of others.

The Rock

Activity: Act of praise
Scripture: Joshua 3:14–4:7
You'll need a large rock, index cards, pens, and tape.

Overview

Throughout the Old Testament, God's people often built monuments to God as a way of praising him for his goodness and as reminders of what God had done.

• In this activity, participants journey into the Old Testament and, like the Israelites, build a monument to remind them of God's goodness.

Bring the largest rock you can move, and set it at the front of your worship area. Consider using a dolly or having some volunteers help you move the rock into your church. If you have a large congregation, you may need more than one rock. Scatter index cards, pens, and rolls of tape around the rock.

At the appropriate time during worship, explain the importance of remembering God's goodness. Then direct the members of your congregation to assemble at the rock. Explain that the congregation will build a monument to serve as a reminder of the wonderful things God has done for your church.

Direct each worshipper to write on an index card at least one way God has blessed his or her life, answered a prayer, or provided help in a time of need. When people are finished, have them tape their index cards to the rock then return to their seats.

(**Note:** If you have a rock that will not accommodate as many cards as you have participants, consider cutting the cards into thirds prior to the activity.)

Keep the monument in a prominent place in your church for at least the next three weeks, and allow church members to add index cards as God answers prayers or brings blessings into their lives.

(**Variation:** Instead of using a rock, consider providing an empty prayer journal for people to log their praise reports in. Have the journal circulate through the congregation as you teach.)

What Are They Looking At?

Activity: Call to worship
Scripture: Mark 2:1-5
You'll need a Bible and ten to fifteen volunteers.

Overview

The excitement surrounding Jesus' ministry must have been tremendous indeed as people were clamoring to get near him and hear his words. Unfortunately, many people today have become apathetic toward Jesus and find the world around them much more exciting.

• This activity helps you address apathy in your church and reminds worshippers of the importance of Christ's teachings.

Prior to the worship service, arrange for ten to fifteen people to serve as volunteers. Ask them to gather near the front of the worship area just before the service as if they are looking at something that captivates their interest. Place an open Bible in front of them to help them focus. Encourage them to remain around the Bible and strain for a better look. (**Note:** Ask your volunteers to act interested but to avoid overacting. Don't be concerned if others join the volunteers.)

As the service is beginning, have the volunteers freeze. Ask the congregation if any of them were interested in what the people up front were looking at. Take a moment to discuss some of the things that pique people's interest in today's society—car wrecks, arguments, and special effects in movies, for example. (**Note:** Rather than listing these yourself, consider asking the congregation to list them, and engage people in a short discussion.)

After a few minutes, read aloud Mark 2:1-5, and remind worshippers that the most exciting, most important, and most interesting subject in the world is right before them—the message of Christ.

(**Variation:** Rather than having several people help you, ask one volunteer to interrupt you and argue with you during your sermon. Make sure you give the volunteer a key phrase to listen for. Get into a verbal disagreement with the volunteer. After a minute or two, inform the congregation about what is really going on, and thank your volunteer. Point out how interested everyone was in the disagreement, and explain how the words of Christ are much more interesting and important.)

Prepare Your Hearts

Activity: Celebration of the Lord's Supper
Scripture: 1 Corinthians 11:23-34
You'll need food for a banquet or potluck meal after the worship service.

Overview
In the days of the early church, the Lord's Supper took place during meals, but it wasn't long until the church in Corinth developed selfish motives and started abusing the Lord's Supper (1 Corinthians 11:20-22). Paul knew that such abuses came from a lack of self-examination and from forgetting that the Lord's Supper is about Christ (1 Corinthians 11:28-29).

• This fasting activity, done prior to worship, will challenge participants to think more deeply and seriously about the Lord's Supper.

A week or two prior to the worship service in which you'll be using this activity, challenge the members of your congregation to fast from after lunch Saturday through Sunday morning breakfast as a way to prepare for a more meaningful Lord's Supper. Promote the fast through bulletins and announcements. Also consider sending a letter to church members during the week as a reminder. In the letter, challenge church members to study 1 Corinthians 11:23-34, and encourage them to examine themselves during the fast as a way to prepare their hearts for the Lord's Supper.

During the worship service, lead the congregation in its regular service of the

Lord's Supper. Afterward hold a banquet or potluck as a way of celebrating the forgiveness and salvation God offers through Christ.

(**Variation:** For a creative way to administer the Lord's Supper, have someone from each family go to the front of the worship area to get the elements. Then have families or friends take the Lord's Supper together.)

When I Consider Your Heavens

Activity: Creative reading, benediction
Scripture: Psalm 8
You'll need Bibles or copies of Psalm 8.

Overview

As David surveyed God's glorious works of creation, he was moved to praise God. We can learn from David and praise God each day for the glories of his kingdom.

• In this activity, worshippers recess outside to get a magnificent view of God's creation as they read Psalm 8 together. This activity is best done at the very end of the service.

At the end of the service, have worshippers take their Bibles and recess outside. As people exit, distribute additional Bibles or copies of Psalm 8 to those who need them.

Once outside, ask everyone to focus on something God created, whether it be a flower, a tree, or even the sky. Say:

> **When David thought about what God had accomplished in creation, he responded with praise for God. As we contemplate the glory of God's creation, let us read Psalm 8 aloud together.**

(**Variation:** If you have clear windows in or near your worship area, you may simply ask worshippers to remain in their seats and focus on God's creation as they read the Psalm.)

With Branches in Their Hands

Activity: Call to worship, creative movement

Scripture: Psalm 118:26-29; Revelation 7:9-10

You'll need Bibles and palm branches, pine boughs, or other greenery for each participant.

Overview

In the book of Revelation, John describes the beautiful scene of Jesus' return as he is greeted by worshippers holding branches in their hands.

• This activity, which takes the form of a march into the worship area, gives worshippers an opportunity to honor and celebrate Jesus in a way much like what will occur upon his return.

Greet people as they arrive, and hand each person a branch. Rather than having the congregation enter the worship area when they arrive, ask everyone to wait in the reception area until just before the service. When it's time for worship to begin, read aloud Psalm 118:26-29 and Revelation 7:9-10, then ask everyone to follow you into the worship area, waving their branches in the air. If your church has a center aisle and two outside aisles, attendees can follow you up to the front, place their branches on or near the worship platform, and walk down the side aisles to take their seats. Have ushers help with traffic control.

Plan to have the choir or congregation sing a joyful hymn of praise during the procession. If the choir sings, have it situated in its usual place in the worship area when the service begins. If the congregation sings, choose a song familiar enough that worshippers won't need written words or music as they're walking in.

The Church in Action

Activity: Offering

Scripture: James 2:14-17

You'll need paper scraps and pens or pencils.

Overview

When James spoke of faith, he didn't ask his readers to enter a musty world of academic philosophy. Instead, he entreated those who profess faith in Christ to do so visibly and practically. The words of James are as relevant today as they were to those early Christians.

• This activity helps worshippers think of tangible ways to make their faith real in their own lives and in the lives of others.

When you are ready to begin, have ushers hand out paper and pens or pencils to all worshippers. Say:

> **Today we'll be accepting a special offering in addition to your regular monetary gift. But instead of asking you to delve deeper into your wallets, our challenge is to look deeper into your lives. Think of an offering of time or effort you can give someone in the coming week. Such activities might include volunteering in a homeless shelter, visiting a shut-in neighbor, or helping a young mother with grocery shopping. This gift of time could even be as simple as vowing to spend some quality time that's been missing with a spouse or children.**
>
> **Let God guide you as you think about what to do. Maybe the Holy Spirit is nudging you to help that cranky neighbor across the street! The gift of time to which you commit should be done personally— no anonymous checks allowed! Commit to the time offering by writing a brief description of your intentions on your piece of paper. No one will examine your commitments; writing your intentions and placing them in the offering is a way of showing God that you'll try to live out your faith in a tangible way this week.**

Follow up next week by asking for a show of hands of those who followed through on their commitments.

(**Variation:** This activity can also be tailored to fit particular situations in your church. For example, make the offering intergenerational by asking each person to commit to doing something for or with someone from a different generation. Or give the offering a missions theme, or tie it to a particular need in your community. And don't forget the kids! Children can commit to simple acts of selflessness too, even if they vow simply to help a sibling pick up toys before bed.)

Greeters, Greeters, and More Greeters

Activity: Pre-service greeting
Scripture: 2 Corinthians 13:12

Overview
Paul illustrates in 2 Corinthians 13:12 that greeting one another is an important part of the Christian faith.

• This activity encourages church members to get out of their comfort zones regarding their relationships and interactions with other church members.

Before worship begins, designate at least two volunteers to serve as greeting facilitators. Have each volunteer stand at the entrance of your church and greet the first people who arrive. Instruct the facilitators to inform the first people they greet that they are now official greeters also. The facilitators should tell the new greeters that they may not sit down until they greet someone else and designate that someone as an official greeter. Instruct the greeting facilitators to direct the process so that everyone has an opportunity to greet at least one person who arrives after him or her.

If you have a very large church, you may want to provide extra facilitators who make certain that everyone is greeted.

During the service, use the greeting experience to talk about how Christians need to reach out to and love one another.

(**Note:** In an effort to be sensitive to visitors, you might consider having regular members accompany them during this activity.)

Prayer Planes

Activity: Benediction, prayer
Scripture: Romans 15:31; James 5:16
You'll need a pencil for each person and an 8 ½x11 sheet of paper folded and

inserted into each bulletin or handed to each person in the worship service at the appropriate time.

Overview

When Paul asked his fellow Christians to pray for him in Romans 15:31, he was well aware of the strength that comes in praying for one another, as was James, who instructs us to "pray for each other" (5:16).

• This activity provides an opportunity to accept the biblical challenge to pray for our fellow brothers and sisters in Christ. It works especially well as a closing prayer.

At the appropriate time, ask each worshipper to take a sheet of paper, write his or her name on it, and—if desired—write a special prayer request. Next have everyone fold the sheet of paper into a paper airplane, or "prayer plane."

(**Note:** This experience can also serve as a very good intergenerational activity. Adults or teenagers can help younger members fold their airplanes, and younger members can help senior members who may have difficulty with this part of the activity.)

Once people have folded the sheets of paper, give the command for the worshippers to float their airplanes through the air. After the prayer planes have landed, have each person pick one up. Explain that the person who picked up the prayer plane will become a prayer partner to the person whose name is written on the it. Challenge the worshippers to pray for their prayer partners throughout the week.

(**Note:** If you use this activity early in the worship service, challenge participants to pray for their partners throughout worship.)

(**Variation:** Rather than making paper airplanes, a lower-risk alternative is to have worshippers write their names and prayer requests on sheets of paper or index cards. Have ushers gather the requests and redistribute them before everyone leaves.)

Humility and Reverence

Activity: Worship posture
Scripture: 2 Chronicles 29:28, 30; Psalm 95:6
You'll need hymnals or printed praise choruses for participants.

Overview

When Hezekiah purified and rededicated the Temple, he led the Israelites in a special time of worship. As a symbol of the Israelites' repentance and humility, they bowed in worship while sacrifices were made and worship music was played.

• This activity helps worshippers demonstrate their humility and reverence to God.

Encourage your congregation to try the following posture of praise in order to move their worship of God to a new level. Be sure everyone has a hymnal, chorus book, or sheet with lyrics printed on it. Inform the congregation that during the musical portions of the service, worshippers will participate with their heads bowed.

Read aloud 2 Chronicles 29:28, 30 and explain that Hezekiah led the Israelites in worshipping with this posture after they had rededicated the Temple in ancient Israel. Ask congregation members to demonstrate their humility and reverence to God during the musical portions of worship by bowing their heads and not looking up.

(**Variation**: Another option is to have the congregation members kneel and bow their heads at the same time. This full-body posture is actually closer to the Old Testament example of bowing down in praise.)

New Wineskins

Activity: Prayer
Scripture: Matthew 9:17
You'll need markers and small pieces of leather.

Overview

As followers of Christ, we must always be prepared for new challenges, including new ways to live and new ways to serve.

• This activity encourages worshippers to embrace change as an important part of their Christian growth.

Read aloud Matthew 9:17, and say:

> **When God wants to do something new in his church, one obstacle he often faces is us. We're comfortable. We're set in our ways. We've lost**

our willingness to make changes that need to be made in a growing relationship with God. Unfortunately for our comfort, we serve a God who expects us to grow through change.

Ask everyone to stand and to move someplace in the room where they don't normally sit. Give people a few moments to get situated in a new spot. Arrange to do this yourself also by moving the speaking stand to a new place in the room.

Say:

It feels a little uncomfortable, doesn't it? And yet all we did was shift about in a very familiar room. Not much of a change when you think about it...but still enough to feel a little odd. What if God asked us to change where we live? To go to a foreign country? To try a new kind of ministry? To give more? To live more? To reach out to others more?

God understands change. God invented it, and he's experienced it. Jesus left glory for the indignity of a stable in Bethlehem. He lived here among us. He traded in the adoration of angels for the jeering of a crowd.

Hold up one of the pieces of leather, and continue:

This piece of leather represents a new wineskin. The new wine of grace wouldn't fit into the old wineskins of the law. So God delivered grace in the person of Jesus Christ.

What changes does God want to make in our church? In our lives? What new wine does he want to pour out? What new wine does he want us to receive?

Distribute pieces of leather and markers.

Say:

Write down one thing God wants you to change in your life or our church. The change might be that you become more tolerant. It might be that you seek healing in a relationship. It might be that our congregation becomes more involved in missions. Whatever it is, take a moment to write it down on your "new wineskins." Afterward take a moment to pray that God will give you—and the church— strength to make the necessary change and to continue to challenge

you in Christian growth.

After a few minutes of silent meditation, offer a corporate prayer. Challenge worshippers to take their "new wineskins" home with them as reminders of the changes they are seeking to make.

Declare God's Glory

Activity: Invocation
Scripture: 1 Chronicles 16:23-34
You'll need a Bible.

Overview

When priests brought the ark of the covenant into Jerusalem, the occasion called for a special celebration. David wrote this Psalm of thanks in honor of that occasion.

• This activity uses a passage of Scripture as a powerful invocation.

Read aloud 1 Chronicles 16:23-34 in a dramatic fashion as an invocation to praise. Follow the invocation with a good opening song such as "Crown Him With Many Crowns" or "Our God Reigns."

(Variation: Use two to six volunteer readers to alternate reading verses aloud.)

No Limit to Forgiveness

Activity: Benediction
Scripture: Luke 6:27-28
You'll need a Bible, small slips of paper, and pencils.

Overview

Jesus taught that there is to be no limit to our forgiveness. God forgives us, and we are to forgive others—even going as far as blessing those who curse us and praying for those who mistreat us.

• In this activity, worshippers each think of someone they need to forgive and pray for God to bless that person.

At the appropriate time, distribute the slips of paper and pencils to all worshippers. Read aloud Luke 6:27-28. Ask worshippers each to think about the person they most need to forgive, whether it be from a time long ago or the present. Instruct worshippers each to write that person's name on the slip of paper.

After a few moments, ask participants each to think about a need or wish that person may have in life such as a new job, a better marriage, or more free time. To help people with this, encourage them to think about hobbies that person may have or about what his or her typical day may be like. Instruct worshippers each to write the need down on their slips of paper.

After a few moments, say:

> **A benediction is usually spoken to God to ask for a blessing on the worshippers. But today we will be asking for God's blessing on those people we most need to forgive. If you aren't sure how to pray for the person, simply offer God the following one-sentence prayer: "Dear God, please bless (name) with (what he or she may want)."**

Allow a minute for silent prayer. Then close with a benediction, praying for the worshippers to take Jesus' words to heart as they seek the true meaning of forgiveness.

Encourage worshippers to put their slips of paper in their Bibles and pray regularly for the people whose names they've written in an effort to forgive.

Worship in the Round

Activity: Act of praise
Scripture: Romans 12:1; 15:5-6
You'll need a Bible and a praise song with which worshippers are familiar or the necessary equipment to project the lyrics on a wall or screen.

Overview
Romans 15:5-6 offers a unity prayer of praise that describes the church as having "one heart and mouth" to glorify God.

- This activity illustrates how we offer praise to God by offering our bodies as living sacrifices.

Ask the congregation to stand, form a large circle around the worship area, and hold hands. As they are doing this, read aloud Romans 12:1 and Romans 15:5-6.

Tell worshippers that as a symbol of their spirit of unity they are going to worship God by singing a song in the round today. Remind worshippers that as they feel the pulse or sweat in the hand of the person next to them, they are touching a living sacrifice.

Worthy of Our Praise

Activity: Call to worship
Scripture: Deuteronomy 10:17a; 32:3; 1 Chronicles 16:25a; 2 Samuel 7:22a; Psalm 47:2; 145:3a; Lamentations 3:22-23; Daniel 9:4b
You'll need eight volunteers with Bibles.

Overview
An important theme that is common in the Old Testament is "Our God is great and worthy of our praise!"

- This activity involves people in a call to worship consisting of several Scripture verses that issue a clear call to praise the greatness of God.

Prior to the worship service, recruit eight volunteers to help with the call to worship. Assign each volunteer one of the Bible verses, and number them in the order you want volunteers to read them. Instruct the helpers to locate themselves in different parts of the worship area as they arrive for worship. Provide a cue so they'll know when to begin the readings. Suggest that they stand as they read. The Scriptures should be read as follows:
- 1 Chronicles 16:25a—"For great is the Lord and most worthy of praise."
- Deuteronomy 10:17a—"For the Lord your God is God of gods and Lord of lords, the great God, mighty and awesome."
- 2 Samuel 7:22a—"How great you are, O Sovereign Lord! There is no one like you, and there is no God but you."

- Psalm 47:2—"How awesome is the Lord Most High, the great King over all the earth!"
- Psalm 145:3a—"Great is the Lord and most worthy of praise."
- Lamentations 3:22-23—"Because of the Lord's great love we are not consumed, for his compassions never fail. They are new every morning; great is your faithfulness."
- Daniel 9:4b—"O Lord, the great and awesome God, who keeps his covenant of love with all who love him and obey his commands."
- Deuteronomy 32:3—"I will proclaim the name of the Lord. Oh, praise the greatness of our God!"

Wonderfully Made

Activity: Creative reading, call to worship
Scripture: Psalm 139:13-14a
You'll need a photocopy of the "Wonderfully Made" handout (p. 29) for each participant (either inserted into bulletins or handed out).

Overview
God's Word teaches us that we should have as much respect for ourselves as the Creator has for us.

- The poem on the handout, which is related to Psalm 139:13-14a, makes a wonderful responsive reading and reminds worshippers that they are "fearfully and wonderfully made."

When you are ready to begin this activity, read aloud Psalm 139:13-14a to the congregation and then lead them in the responsive reading.

WONDERFULLY MADE

Worship Leader: For bones that bind and blood that flows,

All: We praise you, Lord!

Worship Leader: For eyes that see and ears that hear,

All: We praise you, Lord!

Worship Leader: For lungs that breathe and hearts that pound,

Women: We praise you, Lord!

Worship Leader: For feet that step and hands that touch,

Men: We praise you, Lord!

Worship Leader: For minds that think and souls that live,

All: We praise you, Lord!

Story Collage

Activity: Sharing time, meditation

Scripture: James 1:2-5

You'll need a Bible, one large paper or cloth banner at the front of the worship area, one small piece of paper or cloth for each person, pens or cloth markers, and glue sticks or straight pins.

Overview

James instructed Christians to take joy in their hardships because by their faith they are assured that God will give them strength to persevere.

• This activity gives worshippers an opportunity to share and hear about God's work in the lives of people during times of hardship.

At the appropriate time, have ushers distribute a piece of paper or cloth as well as a pen or marker to each person.

Read aloud James 1:2-5, and say:

> **Each person here has undoubtedly gone through at least one or two hardships in life. As we move beyond these times of difficulty, we often can look back and see how God was working to help us endure. As the Scripture says, God often uses these times to strengthen our character. As a way of encouraging each other and bringing praise before God, today I would like you to share some of your stories. Our plan is to create a collage that will show how God is working in our lives.**

Give each person time to write or draw a brief story on the piece of paper or cloth. Invite families or friends to work together if they have shared experiences.

After approximately five minutes, encourage worshippers to bring their pieces of paper or cloth to the front of the worship area and glue or pin their stories to the banner to create a "story collage." If time allows, consider asking a few volunteers to share their stories aloud.

(**Note:** Have ushers gather pieces of paper or cloth from those who might have difficulty bringing them to the front themselves.)

The Heavens Declare the Glory

Activity: Creative reading

Scripture: Psalm 19:1-3

You'll need four photocopies of the "Heavens Declare the Glory" handouts (p. 32), a slide or video projector, slides or video clips of interstellar formations, a screen or blank wall, soft music, a cassette or CD player, and four volunteer readers.

Overview

When we consider the glory of God, we think in terms of what we've experienced ourselves. But God's glory stretches far beyond our daily lives.

• This activity helps worshippers recognize that God's glory reaches far beyond their own limited experience.

To prepare for this activity, visit your local lending library to borrow slides or video resources containing recent Hubble Telescope photos. If your library can't provide these images, download them from the Internet or call area high school or college science departments.

Create a three- to four-minute collage of images, and select an appropriate piece of music such as a soundtrack for this meditation. You'll probably want to use music without lyrics, which might be distracting when your readers speak. Use arrangements that are soft and that might be described as "haunting" or "celestial." Your local lending library can offer help selecting a resource, but one widely available classical option is Mozart's *Divertimento in D, K. 136.*

Prior to worship, recruit four readers. Give each reader a copy of the handout (p. 32). Be sure your readers know to speak clearly and with adequate volume. A rehearsal beforehand might be helpful.

Place readers so they are scattered throughout the room. Instruct them to pause for fifteen seconds between each line. Instruct your first reader not to begin until the visuals have been displayed for thirty seconds.

When you are ready to begin this activity and just before the lights are turned down, say:

The Heavens Declare the Glory

Reader 1: "The heavens declare the glory of God."

Reader 2: "The skies proclaim the work of his hands."

Reader 3: "Day after day they pour forth speech."

Reader 4: "Night after night they display knowledge."

Reader 1: "There is no speech or language where their voice is not heard."

Reader 2: "The heavens declare the glory of God."

Readers 3 and 4: "The heavens declare the glory of God."

Reader 1: "The heavens declare the glory of God."

When we consider the glory of God, we think in terms of what we've experienced ourselves. The rim of the Grand Canyon at sunrise. A baby's first cry. A star-filled sky. But God's glory stretches far beyond our own limited experience. "The heavens declare the glory of God."

Begin the music and slide show.

(**Note:** Be sure to observe appropriate copyright laws when using copyrighted material.)

God's Amazing Grace

Activity: Sharing time, music experience
Scripture: Colossians 1:6b
You'll need a Bible, a traveling microphone, and hymnals that include the song "Amazing Grace" (or lyrics projected on a screen).

Overview

"Amazing Grace" is one of the most inspiring hymns in the English language. By personalizing its message, worshippers can deepen their understanding of God's grace.

• This musical experience will provide an opportunity for worshippers to meditate upon and share what grace has taught each of them individually.

Begin by having the congregation sing the first two verses of "Amazing Grace." Instruct the instrumental accompaniment to continue playing softly in the background.

Read aloud Colossians 1:6, and say:

As the music of "Amazing Grace" continues, I want you to spend a few minutes thinking of ways that God's grace has changed your life. In a moment I will be wandering around with a microphone and will ask for a few volunteers to share some of their stories and thoughts.

Allow the instruments to play through a full verse as participants think. Then ask for a few volunteers to share their stories.

After a few worshippers have shared, ask the congregation to join in singing the remaining verses of the song together. To conclude, have the congregation sing the first verse without musical accompaniment.

God Knows Our Every Need

Activity: Prayer
Scripture: Matthew 6:8; Romans 8:26-27
You'll need a Bible.

Overview

These Scriptures remind us that God knows what we need before we ask him. What a wonderful feeling to know that even when we are confused or don't know what to pray for, God is aware of our needs.

• In this activity, worshippers attempt to communicate with one another without using words and will pray for one another.

Ask worshippers to think about something they need to pray about. After a moment of silent reflection, have participants turn to a partner. Challenge them to explain the prayer need to their partner *without using any words*. They may motion with their hands, eyes, heads, or feet, but may not use words—written or spoken.

After two or three minutes of silent sharing, read aloud Romans 8:26-27 and Matthew 6:8. Conclude the activity by asking worshippers to pray for their partners with the knowledge that whether or not they understood the prayer need, God is already aware of it.

Breaking the Comfort Zone

Activity: Pre-service greeting
Scripture: Exodus 3:11; Hebrews 11

Overview

God wanted Moses to lead Israel out of Egypt, but Moses balked at the idea because it took him well beyond his comfort zone. Sometimes, however, faith requires us to break out of our normal routines and step out of our comfort zones.

• Use this activity to challenge worshippers to sit in seats different from where they usually sit in an effort to break out of their comfort zones.

As people enter the worship area, greet them warmly and ask them to sit in seats different from their usual ones. You may even want to direct some worshippers to specific unusual seats, such as those at the front of the worship area, in the choir area, with the musicians, or even next to the pulpit or platform from which you speak.

When worshippers are seated, begin speaking from the back of the worship area. Say:

> **Today's seating arrangement will help us move out of our comfort zones. I challenge you to stay in these unusual seats for the worship service, and as you do, to notice how it makes you feel. Sometimes we get too settled—even stuck—in our usual way of doing things. When we're working for God, sometimes we have to do things that are neither normal nor comfortable for us.**

Continue with the service as planned.

(**Variation:** Consider carrying this theme through the service by having worshippers do things differently from how they usually do things. For example, if you normally stand while singing, sit instead; if you normally bow your heads while praying, look up or hold your hands in the air.)

Encouraging One Another

Activity: Benediction
Scripture: Hebrews 10:24
You'll need a stamped postcard for each participant and pens or pencils.

Overview

The writer of Hebrews reminds us to encourage one another in love and good deeds.

- This activity provides a good closing to a worship service and a way to encourage others in their Christian faith.

Just prior to the benediction, have ushers distribute stamped postcards. Ask participants to do one of two things with the postcards:
- Write words of encouragement about something they have observed another member doing that has not been publicly recognized.
- Make a "coupon" good for a specific act of kindness, such as an evening of baby-sitting or a meal at a favorite restaurant—your treat!

Have worshippers each write the recipient's name on the back of the postcard. Offer to collect the postcards to be addressed and mailed by church staff, or let people take them home and mail them. Be sure to allow enough time for everyone to complete the activity prior to the benediction or closing prayer.

The Sheep of His Pasture

Activity: Invocation
Scripture: Psalm 100:1-3
You'll need a Bible and photocopies of the "Smiley Sheep" handout (p. 37).

Overview
Psalm 100 challenges worshippers to enter joyfully into God's presence.

- This passage of Scripture serves as a wonderful invocation and sets the stage for a joyful attitude in worship.

Have the ushers distribute copies of the "Smiley Sheep" handout (p. 37) to participants. Encourage worshippers to take their handouts home and post them in a conspicuous place to remind them to worship God with gladness and joy.

Read aloud Psalm 100:1-3, present the invocation, and then follow it with a joyful song such as "Joyful, Joyful We Adore Thee" or "The Joy of the Lord Is My Strength."

Smiley Sheep

I will "worship the Lord with gladness" (Psalm 100:2).

God Loves a Hilarious Giver

Activity: Offering

Scripture: 2 Corinthians 9:7

You'll need a Bible.

Overview

Paul called the Corinthians to maintain an attitude of joyful giving. His words challenge us today to have the same attitude of cheerful or "hilarious" giving. The English word "hilarious" comes from the Greek word *hilaros,* which is translated as "cheerful."

• This activity encourages worshippers to give joyfully and "hilariously."

If possible, begin a preoffering meditation by telling a suitable joke. Ask the congregation what it feels like to laugh at a hilarious joke. Call attention to their laughter and the joy that comes from it. Ask:

> **How is the joy that comes from laughter like the feelings we experience when we joyfully give our tithes and offerings?**

After receiving a few responses to the question, read aloud 2 Corinthians 9:7. Explain that the English word "hilarious" comes from a Greek word that's translated as "cheerful." Encourage the congregation to practice laughing with you. You might need to tell another appropriate joke to set the stage. Once they've stopped laughing, have the ushers pass the offering plate, and encourage worshippers to give joyfully as they remember that God loves a cheerful giver.

An Answer to Prayer

Activity: Prayer, sharing time

Scripture: Galatians 6:2

You'll need newsprint, tape, markers, and pens.

Overview

Christians should not believe that they are completely independent and don't need help from others. We are at our best when we work together, support each other, and share in each other's burdens. In this way, according to Paul, we "fulfill the law of Christ."

• This activity gives your church members a practical opportunity to "carry each other's burdens." It also helps worshippers see the power of prayer at work.

Prior to the service, you'll need to make four banners. Each banner should clearly list one of the following areas of concern: finances, relationships, time/stress, faith/relationship with God. You can generate the banners on a computer, have a copy store create them for you, or simply write each one on a separate sheet of newsprint. Be sure to leave enough room on your banners for people to write on them. Tape the sheets to different areas of your worship area.

When it's time to address prayer needs, direct the members of your congregation to stand near the banners that most closely match their current needs or concerns. Once they've gathered at the appropriate banners, have participants form groups of three to share their needs and pray for each other.

After a few minutes, ask the worshippers to return to their seats. Explain that you will leave the banners up for the next six weeks. Challenge the congregation members to write answered prayers on the newsprint every time one of their prayer concerns is met. Over the next six weeks, continue having people pray for each other, and encourage the members of your congregation to examine the sheets from time to time.

(**Variation:** The four suggested prayer stations in the activity are a great place to start. But consider making more focused and specialized stations for your congregation. For example, you could break the relationships category into the following stations: parents, children, friends, coworkers, spouses, other relatives. Each category can be as general or specific as you deem necessary.)

All God's Children

Activity: Sharing time
Scripture: Galatians 3:26-27; Ephesians 4:2-6
You'll need a Bible.

Overview
In biblical times, as today, there were divisions in the church. Paul instructed

members of the church body to see beyond divided philosophies, to seek unity, and to treat each other as God's children.

• In this activity, worshippers will to discover experiences, traits, and opinions that they have in common with each other.

Ask the worshippers in each row or area (no more than eight worshippers per group) to find something they all have in common. Encourage them to look beyond simple solutions such as "We're all at church today" and discover common experiences, traits, or opinions. For example, one group may learn that they all prefer living in the country as opposed to the city. (This experience is also a very interesting intergenerational activity as people of all ages find that they have things in common.)

After allowing a few minutes of sharing, ask for a volunteer from each group to report what group members discovered they have in common. Emphasize that the greatest thing they all have in common is a belief in Christ, which makes them all children of God's family.

To conclude, read aloud Galatians 3:26-27 or Ephesians 4:2-6, and ask group members to take a few more minutes to discuss how their common bonds can positively affect how they care for each other.

Working in Harmony

Activity: Music experience, meditation
Scripture: 1 Corinthians 12:24b-26

Overview
Christians have all been given special and unique gifts from God. When they use these gifts and work together, the whole church can accomplish great things for God's kingdom.

• In this activity, worshippers sing together to illustrate the beautiful harmony created when members of Christ's body work together.

Say:

> We are going to do an experiment in worship that will illustrate what happens when members of the church use their unique gifts to work together.

Indicate three sections of worshippers. Ask the organist or another musician to play a middle C, and then have the first section hum a middle C in response. Then ask the musician to play an E, and ask the second section to hum. Then ask the musician to play an F, and ask the third section to hum. Finally have all three sections hum their notes at the same time. For additional fun, have participants change their humming to "ooh," then "ah," then "la, la, la."

Afterward say:

> You're all singing something different, but you're working together in harmony. In the same way, when we put our unique gifts together, we are in harmonious relationship with one another and with God's kingdom. God can accomplish much through a group of Christians who are all in harmony.

Conclude by having the congregation sing a well-known chorus or hymn a cappella.

Memories

Activity: Meditation
Scripture: Joshua 1:1-9
You'll need a Bible and various memory-joggers such as a Christmas CD and CD player, cologne or potpourri, candy, a movie clip and VCR, a painting, or feathers (try to find one item related to each of the five senses).

Overview
Moses had recently died, and Joshua was about to lead Israel through the trying process of moving into the Promised Land. God's promise to be faithful proved true for Joshua and will prove true for the members of your church.

- This activity not only helps the members of your congregation reflect on how God has always been with them, but also challenges them to remember that God will continue to be with them.

Tell worshippers that you're going to use several items to try to jog their memories. Pass the items around and have worshippers look for a moment at each one. After they have heard, smelled, tasted, seen, or touched each memory-jogger, instruct them to close their eyes and think of a *significant* memory from their past that's related to the item.

Then ask your congregation members to think about how God was at work in the event. Repeat the process for each memory-jogger as time allows. Afterward, consider asking a few volunteers to share their memories and to explain how God was at work during the events.

End the meditation by reading aloud Joshua 1:1-9. Say:

> **Just as God promised to be with Joshua, God is with us during both good times and bad times. Even before you came to know Christ, God loved you, protected you, and called you to himself.**

(**Variation:** After participants think about each memory-jogger, have five to ten people share their memories. Highlight the fact that the same object brought very different memories and emotions to mind for each person. Remind people that God meets us where we are in life.)

Cast All Your Cares

Activity: Offering
Scripture: Matthew 11:28-29; 1 Peter 5:7
You'll need a Bible, wide rubber bands, and pens.

Overview

Jesus himself tells us that those who are weary can find rest in him. Peter reminds us that we can believe Jesus' promise to carry our anxiety.

• In this activity, worshippers use rubber bands to symbolically "cast" their anxieties on Jesus.

Just before the offering, distribute rubber bands and pens. Explain that in addition to the regular offering, you want everyone to consider offering something extra today. Read aloud Matthew 11:28-29. Remind worshippers that Jesus asks us to cast all our anxieties on him because he cares for us.

Ask worshippers each to write on the rubber band a word or symbol that represents their anxiety. This could be a specific thing they're worried about or something that is related to the general anxiety they feel. Someone who is worried about a friend or family member might write that person's name on the rubber band.

Stand out of the way, and then ask worshippers to symbolically cast their anxieties on Jesus by shooting their rubber bands toward the front of the worship area. Encourage everyone to aim high so they don't hit anyone.

(**Note:** You may want to have worshippers shoot their rubber bands section by section, with everyone sitting down except for the section shooting. Or you could have small groups of worshippers approach the front of the worship area and shoot their rubber bands only a short distance.)

After the participants have finished "casting their burdens," read aloud 1 Peter 5:7. Then close the activity with prayer.

Ripple Effects

Activity: Creative movement
Scripture: 1 Timothy 4:16

Overview
Paul advised Timothy to live with an awareness of how his behavior affected others.

• In this activity, worshippers do the "wave" to illustrate the ripple effect of their behavior on others.

At the appropriate time, tell worshippers that they're going to do the "wave." Assign one person as a starting point, and ask that person to stand with his or her arms in the air and then sit down. Then explain that as soon as the first person's arms are in the air, the second person should begin standing with his or her arms in the air. Worshippers should continue with the exercise until everyone has participated.

Have worshippers practice the wave until they achieve a fairly smooth motion. Then, if you have time, challenge them to do the wave from the beginning to the end, and then from the end back to the beginning.

Use this illustration to point out how our behavior can have either positive or negative "ripple effects" on those around us.

Rest—A Gift From Above

Activity: Prayer, meditation

Scripture: Genesis 2:2-3; Exodus 20:8-11; Matthew 11:28-30

You'll need a Bible, small pillows, and an alarm clock.

Overview

God provides us with times of rest not only for physical and mental refreshment, but also so we will take time to reflect on the glory of his kingdom.

• This quiet, meditative activity helps participants remember that God gives us spiritual and physical rest for a purpose.

Distribute pillows, and ask worshippers to find a comfortable place where they can lie down and relax. If you have a large group of people, simply ask worshippers to keep their eyes closed for the meditation.

Read aloud Genesis 2:2-3. Say:

Physical and spiritual rest are gifts from God. Rest was given to us not only so we may take a break from work, but also so we can take time to celebrate God's glory. Take a moment to think about a time you worked very strenuously and were in need of rest.

Read aloud Exodus 20:8-11. Say:

The Lord created the Sabbath for *everyone,* including men, women, foreigners, animals, and even the land itself. Take a moment to think about someone you know who is in need of peace and rest.

Read aloud Matthew 11:28-30. Say:

Because Jesus has freed us from the burden of our sins, we can find peace and rest in him. Jesus gives us not only physical rest from our labor and emotional rest from stress, but also eternal rest for our souls. Reflect upon a time Jesus gave you comfort.

Sometimes in the midst of our busy lives, we forget that God gives us rest to refresh our bodies and minds. But God also gives us times of rest so that we will reflect on his glory. Take five minutes to rest now. If you prefer, you can use the time to pray. I will set an alarm

which will go off in five minutes.

Conclude the activity by reminding worshippers that a few minutes of prayer and rest each day will rejuvenate them spiritually, physically, and mentally.

Bonded Through Commitment

Activity: Prayer
Scripture: Philippians 1:3-14
You'll need a Bible and, for each worshipper, one small Christian keepsake.

Overview

Paul tells us that even though political situations may separate us, we can be united as the body of Christ through prayer.

• This activity gives worshippers an opportunity to pray for fellow Christians who live in oppressed countries.

When you are ready to begin, have ushers distribute the keepsakes.

Say:

> **In this area of the world, we generally have the freedom to practice our faith in public as a body of Christ. But there are places in the world where Christians are ostracized and are not allowed to worship publicly. Hang on to your keepsakes to remind you of fellow Christians in other countries to whom you are bonded through your commitment to Christ.**

Read aloud Philippians 1:3-14. Say:

> **Paul prayed continually for other Christians while he was in prison to show his love for them and to strengthen their faith.**

> **Take a moment now to silently pray for the persecuted Christians who live in other nations. Pray that the peace of Christ will be shared with those who are keeping Christians from worshipping God.**

After the prayer, say:

Carry your keepsakes with you either in your pocket or your purse. Whenever you pick it up or see it, take a moment to pray for Christians around the world who are persecuted and who are not free to worship God.

Consider It Pure Joy

Activity: Benediction
Scripture: James 1:2-4
You'll need several empty bottles of Joy dishwashing liquid, index cards, and pens.

Overview

James indicates that we should consider our trials pure joy. We can only accomplish this, however, when we are able to get a new perspective on the value of perseverance.

• This activity provides a lighthearted way to look at the potential benefits of a specific burden or trial.

Prior to worship set up the dishwashing bottles at the back of the worship area. Just before the end of the service, have your ushers distribute index cards and pens. Say:

> **Think of a particular trial you are facing in your life right now. Write it on the top of your index card, and then draw a square around it.**

Pause for a moment to allow time for worshippers to complete this portion of the activity, then continue:

> **Draw a circle in the center of the card, and write the word "perseverance" inside it. Next, draw a line from the square to the circle. The line illustrates that perseverance and trials are truly connected, whether we like it or not. Next, on the same side of the card, list four areas of Christian maturity you would like to grow in your life.**

> **Finally, draw a dotted line between the circle and each of the words you listed.**

Pause, then continue:

> **Each dotted line represents a connection you can choose to make from perseverance to maturity. Look at your card, and pray that**

God will give you the courage to make the connection.

You may wish to lead a corporate prayer as the congregation members are praying individually.

Point out that at the back of the worship area are Joy dishwashing liquid bottles. As worshippers leave, have them roll their index cards into tubes that will fit through the tops of the bottles.

Say:

Leaving your cards in the Joy bottles will be a reminder to consider your trials all...Joy!

Faithful to His Promises

Activity: Sharing time

Scripture: Psalm 145:13b

You'll need the words of Psalm 145:13b printed on the inside of worship bulletins, or projected on a screen in the worship area—on two lines like this:

**"The Lord is faithful to all his promises
And loving toward all he has made" (Psalm 145:13b).**

Overview

God's promises are revealed to us in the Bible and have specific application to each of our lives. Sharing with one another the ways we have seen God fulfill his promises strengthens our trust that he will fulfill his promises in the future.

• This activity provides an opportunity to share and rejoice in God's faithfulness.

Decide ahead of time whether you will do this sharing time as an open-microphone activity or whether you will ask specific individuals to share. The object is to have participants share their memories of events in their lives in which it was obvious that God kept promises.

During the worship service, explain to the congregation that after each person shares, he or she should end with the words, "God is faithful to all his promises." Then have the rest of the congregation respond, "And loving toward all he has made."

Colorful Thanksgiving

Activity: Prayer, sharing time
Scripture: Psalm 149:1
You'll need a Bible.

Overview

God gave us the tremendous ability to perceive tiny variations of color, and the many different colors around us can spark unique praise for God's goodness.

• This creative prayer activity emphasizes praising the Lord in a unique way as worshippers praise God with their eyes wide open.

Just prior to the prayer, read aloud Psalm 149:1. Say:

> **Look around the worship area and find a color that reminds you of something in nature which you can thank God for. After you have located a color, take a moment to give thanks.**

Pause.

> **Next look around to find a color that reminds you of something in your heritage that you can thank God for. Afterward take a moment to again offer thanks to God.**

Pause.

> **Now find a color that reminds you of something that gives you joy, and again take a moment to thank God.**

Pause.

> **Find a color that makes you think of someone you know who is in need of prayer. Pray for that person.**

Pause.

> **Finally look around to find a color that represents a particular prayer need you have. Turn to a partner, and take a moment to share your prayer need and how your color represents it. After you have shared, take a moment to pray for each other.**

Fearfully and Wonderfully

Activity: Meditation
Scripture: Psalm 139:14-16
You'll need a Bible, a CD player, and various CDs.

Overview

By acknowledging the omniscience of God, the psalmist reminds us that God knows and understands everything about us. We are "fearfully and wonderfully made."

• This activity uses various musical pieces to help worshippers better understand that God intentionally created us with emotions. It works well as a meditation or is appropriate to launch a sermon about emotions.

Ask worshippers to close their eyes while you play the most exciting piece of music you can find. After playing the piece, ask:

What emotions did you feel as you listened to this piece?

Repeat this process with music that is

- peaceful,
- mellow,
- grating and irritating, and
- comical or rambunctious.

After each piece, ask the listeners what emotions it evoked.

Afterward, read aloud Psalm 139:14-16. Challenge worshippers to acknowledge that it is natural for us to experience a variety of emotions because God created us with them. Emotions are nothing to be ashamed of.

(**Variation:** Consider using this meditation to teach congregation members about the need for musical variety in worship. After each piece is played, ask for an honest show of hands from those who liked the piece, who didn't like it, and who could take it or leave it. Point out that a variety of music is needed to meet the worship needs of a typical congregation.)

His Body, Broken

Activity: Celebration of the Lord's Supper
Scripture: Exodus 12:12-14; Matthew 26:17-29
You'll need Bibles and four volunteers to read Scripture.

Overview

When God called his people out of Egypt, he instructed them to place lamb's blood over their doorframes to identify them as God's chosen people and to protect them from death. Jesus fulfilled the Passover in his death; he became the lamb who protects us from eternal death and separation from God.

• This activity reminds participants of the meaning of the Passover and its connection to the celebration of the Lord's Supper.

Prior to worship, assign one of the following Scriptures to each volunteer, and instruct the volunteers when they are to read Exodus 12:12-14; Matthew 26:17-19; Matthew 26:20-26; and Matthew 26:27-29.

At the appropriate time, say:

> When the Israelites were slaves in Egypt, God called them to leave and go to the Promised Land. When Pharaoh refused to let the Israelites leave, God brought judgment on Egypt through plagues. The final plague was the death of the firstborn in each family. God announced a way to redeem his people. Each family was to kill a lamb, eat the meat along with some bread made without yeast, and spread the blood of the lamb over the doorframe of the house.

Have the first volunteer read aloud Exodus 12:12-14.

Say:

> And so the Israelites were spared the death of their firstborn, and they were redeemed from slavery in Egypt. For generations, they celebrated the Feast of the Passover to commemorate their deliverance through the blood of the lamb.
>
> Jesus and his disciples celebrated the Passover together on the night Jesus was betrayed. That night, the disciples came to understand that

Jesus himself was the true lamb and would shed his own blood for the deliverance of all who believed in him. Today we celebrate the Lord's Supper in remembrance of Jesus' broken body and shed blood.

Have the second volunteer read aloud Matthew 26:17-19. Pause while the elements for the Lord's Supper are distributed. After the elements have been distributed, have the third volunteer read aloud Matthew 26:20-26. Pause, then direct everyone to eat the bread. Continue by having the fourth volunteer read aloud Matthew 26:27-29. Ask everyone to drink the cup together. Afterward, say:

And so Jesus became our Passover lamb. His blood was shed so that we might be delivered from slavery to sin and death. His body was broken so we might be redeemed. Rejoice! Jesus is the lamb of God!

Gather Together

Activity: Call to worship, music experience
Scripture: Psalm 24:1-3
You'll need Bibles, copies of the hymn "We Gather Together" (commonly available in many hymnals), and three volunteer readers.

Overview
Psalm 24 reminds us that everything belongs to God and that we should worship him and welcome the glories of God's kingdom.

• This activity combines a Scripture reading with a traditional hymn as a bold but beautiful call to worship.

Before worship, assign each of the three verses to a volunteer reader.

Begin the call to worship by having the first reader read aloud Psalm 24:1. Immediately afterward, lead the congregation in singing the first stanza of "We Gather Together."

Next have the second reader read aloud the second verse. Then lead the congregation in singing the second stanza of the hymn.

Finally have the third reader read aloud the third verse. Conclude the call to worship by inviting everyone to stand and leading them in singing the third stanza of the hymn.

Wisdom and Godly Living

Activity: Benediction

Scripture: Proverbs 16

You'll need Bibles and slips of paper with individual verse references from Proverbs 16 written on each (duplicate enough so every worshipper will have one).

Overview

Proverbs was written to impart wisdom for godly living. This book of the Bible teaches that all who seek wisdom will benefit greatly.

• This activity makes the Scriptures more personal by adding worshippers' names to the verses and challenges worshippers to respond to God's Word as they prepare to leave.

As worshippers arrive for the service, have ushers give each person a slip of paper on which you've written a verse reference from Proverbs 16. At the appropriate time, direct participants to find the verses in their Bibles and prepare to read their passages. Say:

> **The object of this activity is to read your assigned passage. The idea, however, is to insert your name somewhere in the verse. For example, for Proverbs 16:16 you might read "How much better it is for Tracy to get wisdom than gold, to choose understanding rather than silver!" Let us begin with verse 1.**

If duplicate verses were handed out, have all the participants who were given a matching verse stand and read it in unison. If you have fewer worshippers than the verses in the passage, let each person read more than one verse.

Afterward, challenge the worshippers to put their verse into practice during the week.

I Will Sing Praise to the Name

Activity: Music experience

Scripture: Psalm 7:17

You'll need a Bible, pens or pencils, and index cards.

Overview

Psalms teaches us a great deal about having an attitude of worship. King David, for example, took time to sing praises to God whether he was in trouble and suffering injustice or whether things were going well in his life. We, too, need to learn to be grateful in all circumstances and give thanks to God by singing praises to his name.

• In this activity, each worshipper chooses a Christian hymn, song, or chorus that encourages him or her. The object is to include all the selected musical pieces as part of worship over the next few weeks.

Begin by reading aloud Psalm 7:17. Say:

> **King David wrote this psalm during a time of significant evil and injustice. As you read his other psalms, it becomes obvious that no matter what was going on in David's life—whether it was a time of suffering or a time of blessing—he was always ready to sing praises to God. We, too, can learn from David to "sing praise to the name of the Lord Most High" no matter what is happening in our lives.**

Invite ushers to give an index card and a pen or pencil to each worshipper. Instruct each worshipper to choose a favorite hymn, chorus, or contemporary Christian song that has great meaning to his or her Christian faith and write the name of the song on the card. Below the title, have the person also write a sentence or two that tells why the song has great meaning.

After participants have finished, have ushers collect all the cards. Explain that the plan is to include all the chosen songs in worship during the next few weeks.

If you include the hymn or song numbers as part of a worship bulletin, include a short note telling who picked the song and why it has special meaning for that person. If you write the lyrics on an overhead, consider announcing who chose the song and why.

(**Variation:** If your congregation is small, hold a single service in which you give everyone an opportunity to pick a favorite hymn.)

God Is Changing Us

Activity: Sharing time, prayer

Scripture: 2 Corinthians 3:13-18

You'll need a beach ball.

Overview

Through the power of the Holy Spirit, Christians find the freedom to change and become more Christlike. A heavy burden is removed when we learn to trust Christ to save us.

• This activity involves your church to share the ways in which God is changing us into his likeness. Use the activity just prior to prayer or as a separate time of sharing.

Before the service, blow up a large beach ball. At the appropriate time, explain that God is changing us into his likeness. Hold up the beach ball and share one way you have been changed as a Christian. Then throw the ball out to the congregation. Ask the person who catches the ball to share one way he or she has been changed. Then have that person throw the beach ball to another person.

Continue this process for as long as you like, and end by thanking God for the powerful changes that have occurred and are occurring.

(**Variation:** Instead of using a beach ball, you could use paper airplanes or a Frisbee disc. If you use paper airplanes, be creative and write messages or questions for members of your congregation to read or answer before they share.)

The Best We Have

Activity: Offering

Scripture: Psalm 66:13-15; Hebrews 13:15-16

You'll need a Bible and a receptacle with which to receive a food offering.

Overview

God wants us to give our very best rather than withholding it for ourselves. God wants us to use the blessings we have to meet the needs of others.

- This activity provides an opportunity for worshippers to give to God the "best" fruits of their labor in a food offering. It impresses upon worshippers that God deserves nothing but the best they have to offer.

Prior to the worship service, challenge the congregation to bring a food item that represents the *best* of their garden's harvest or favorite groceries from the store. Possibilities include fresh produce or canned, dried, or baked goods. Children can be urged to donate their favorite candy.

When you are ready to begin this activity, read aloud Psalm 66:13-15 and Hebrews 13:15-16. Say:

> **In biblical times sacrifices were given to God as a way to give thanks, ask for his forgiveness and blessing, and make atonement for their sin. Typically, animals, grains, fruit, and spices were given. Although Jesus' own sacrifice erased the need for us to "pay" for our sins, God still desires that we lay our best gifts before him and to provide for the needs of others.**

During the time of offering, ask worshippers to bring their offerings to the altar. After the service, deliver the food to a local food pantry, safe house, or homeless shelter.

Praise Every Day

Activity: Prayer
Scripture: Psalm 145:1-2
You'll need a Bible, pencils or pens, and index cards.

Overview
The psalmist challenges us to praise and extol God every day, not just during Sunday worship.

- This activity challenges worshippers to make time throughout the week to praise God, despite their busy schedules.

Following a time of prayer, read aloud Psalm 145:1-2. Say:

> **David made a commitment to praise God every day, not just once in**

a while. God's Word challenges us to do the same. We need to take time out of our busy schedules to praise God and give him thanks.

Distribute the index cards and pens or pencils. Ask worshippers to take a moment to decide a specific time to pray each day during the next week. Have each participant write his or her name, phone number, and committed time of prayer on an index card. Then have participants exchange cards with another worshipper. Challenge everyone to call the person on the card at least a couple of times during the week and remind him or her to keep the "appointment" with God.

Suggest that people call their partners either the night before (as doctors' offices often do) or a few minutes prior to the scheduled time.

My Heart Leaps for Joy

Activity: Sharing time
Scripture: Psalm 28:7
You'll need a Bible, pens or pencils, and enough scrap paper for each person to have one sheet.

Overview
The psalmist reminds us that our hearts should leap for joy because of God's promises of protection and blessing.

• This activity encourages worshippers to acknowledge their own blessings and to thank God for the blessings others have received.

Read aloud Psalm 28:7. Have worshippers think about and meditate upon the last time their heart leaped for joy because of something God did in their lives. After a few moments, ask participants to pair up with another worshipper and take a minute to share their joyful blessings as the ushers distribute paper and pens or pencils.

After a few minutes of sharing, have each worshipper write a simple psalm or prayer thanking God for the good thing that happened to his or her partner. Suggest that participants' psalms be limited to five or six lines in length, and remind them that the lines needn't rhyme.

After approximately five minutes, ask for volunteers to stand (or come to the microphone) and read aloud the psalms they wrote for their partners.

In closing, have partners exchange psalms so they can keep the psalms that were written for them.

Waiting to Be Found

Activity: Prayer, call to worship
Scripture: Matthew 7:7-8
You'll need a Bible and, for each worshipper, a piece of card stock with a Bible promise such as those found in Psalm 91:14; Jeremiah 23:5-6; Micah 4:3-4; and Matthew 18:19-20 printed on it (many Christian book stores and gift stores sell "promise cards").

Overview
Jesus repeatedly promises to reveal himself (and, therefore, God) to anyone who sincerely wants to know him.

• This activity uses hidden Bible promise cards to challenge worshippers to take a moment to search for God's promises.

Hide the promise cards in the pew Bibles or near another appropriate place where worshippers will be sitting. As a call to worship, or just prior to prayer, read aloud Matthew 7:7-8. Say:

> **The Scriptures remind us that God delights in giving good gifts to those who seek him and persist in prayer. Even when we don't clearly sense God's presence, God is near.**

Hold up one of the promise cards, and read it aloud. Say:

> **Somewhere in the immediate space around you, a promise card has been hidden for each person. Take a few moments to look around and find a card.**

Pause for a moment while worshippers search.

> **Like these promise cards, God can always be "found," but we often have to persistently seek him. Spend a few minutes now in silence as you meditate upon the ways in which God is waiting for you to discover him.**

57

The New Has Come!

Activity: Benediction, prayer

Scripture: Nehemiah 9:1-3; Luke 10:13; 2 Corinthians 5:17; 1 John 1:8-9

You'll need a Bible, a few pieces of charcoal, and two or three assistants.

Overview

The Bible describes that in an act of repentance, the Israelites would often rub ashes on themselves. Like the Israelites, we, too, need to regularly come before God in acts of repentance.

• This activity gives worshippers an opportunity to participate in an Old Testament tradition of repentance.

Just prior to prayer, read aloud Nehemiah 9:1-3 and Luke 10:13. Challenge worshippers to take a moment to reflect upon something they regret they have done or have left undone during the past week.

After a few moments, say:

> **The Old Testament custom of wearing sackcloth and ashes was a tradition the Israelites used to express sorrow for their sins. Today we are providing an opportunity for those who would like to participate in this biblical tradition and symbolic act of repentance. In a moment you will be invited to come to the front of the worship area and take a moment to silently ask for God's forgiveness. As you do, one of the assistants will place a dot of charcoal on the back of your hand. Then you can return to your seat.**

Have worshippers come forward one row at a time. If necessary, ask ushers to assist with this. After everyone has had an opportunity to come forward, read aloud 2 Corinthians 5:17 and 1 John 1:8-9. Say:

> **It's not the act of putting ashes on your hand that cleanses you; rather it's Christ who forgives all your sins.**

Close with a benediction.

Holy Land Pilgrimage

Activity: Creative movement

Scripture: Exodus 20:1-17; Matthew 4:18-22; Mark 1:7-11; Acts 9:1-19

You'll need Bibles; Bible character costumes; several children or teenage volunteers; and props to depict the events that occurred at Mount Sinai, at the Sea of Galilee, at the Jordan River, and on the road to Damascus, as recorded in the Scripture verses listed above. (For example, use poster board to create "stone tablets" with the Ten Commandments written on them, a large woven hammock to represent fishing nets, a pitcher of water and a bowl to represent the baptism of Jesus, and construction paper on which to draw "fish scales" to cover Saul's eyes.)

Overview

During the Middle Ages, Christians around the world placed much emphasis on participating in pilgrimages to the Holy Land. Even today pilgrimages remain a wonderful way to learn about biblical times.

• This activity allows worshippers to go on an imaginary Bible journey and makes the biblical events seem more real and relevant. The activity will require some preparation.

In preparation for this creative worship pilgrimage, recruit children and teenage volunteers to portray the characters and act out the central themes of each Scripture listed above. Volunteers' outfits needn't be elaborate. Before worship begins, use the four Bible scenes to set up a different station in each corner of the worship area so congregation members can go on a "pilgrimage" to the Holy Land.

Begin by having people form a line and walk in one direction past the different Bible stations. Instruct worshippers to walk slowly by, without talking, as the "actors" read aloud the Scripture passages that represents their scenes.

After worshippers have made their pilgrimage, quiz them to see if they can name the people, places, and events they visited.

Serving With Humility

Activity: Celebration of the Lord's Supper
Scripture: Mark 9:33-35; John 13:12-15; 1 Corinthians 12:7-11
You'll need a Bible and, for each person, an old towel or rag to be handed out with a worship program or placed at each seat.

Overview

Throughout his ministry, Jesus stressed the importance of serving others, then set the example by insisting on washing his disciples' feet during their last meal together.

• This activity provides worshippers with an opportunity to humble themselves and, in so doing, more fully appreciate Jesus' actions and admonition regarding Christian service.

Immediately following a celebration of the Lord's Supper, read aloud John 13:12-15. Invite participants to ask one of the individuals sitting beside them if they may polish his or her shoes (using the rags you've supplied). Encourage everyone to *offer* to serve someone else and to *accept* the service being offered.

Next read aloud Mark 9:33-35 and 1 Corinthians 12:7-11. Follow the Scripture reading by challenging worshippers to think of concrete things they can do to serve someone in need. Allow two or three minutes for quiet reflection, then close with a prayer for discernment and strength for the worshippers.

Enter the Narrow Gate

Activity: Creative movement
Scripture: Psalm 118:20; Matthew 7:13-14; John 10:1-3
You'll need a Bible.

Overview

The Bible reminds us that Jesus is the gate that leads to eternal life. This gate is the only entrance into eternal life.

- This activity creatively reminds worshippers that Jesus is the gate through which we may enter the kingdom of heaven.

Read aloud Matthew 7:13-14 and John 10:1-3. Ask worshippers to stand in the aisles, and then request that every other person find a partner with whom he or she can form a "gate." Explain that this is accomplished by holding their arms over their heads, extended slightly forward, and by joining hands with someone else.

Once the "gates" are in place, instruct the remaining worshippers to walk beneath them until you call "time out." Consider having an appropriate musical piece played in the background during this time, or invite worshippers to sing a hymn or praise song.

Have everyone pause for a moment, then read aloud Psalm 118:20. Have members of the congregation switch roles and repeat the process.

After all the worshippers have had an opportunity to walk through a gate, have them return to their seats. Say:

Jesus reminds us that the gate that leads to eternal life is narrow. In other words, there is only one way to live eternally with God. Take a moment now to thank God for calling you to walk through his gate.

On Your Hand

Activity: Benediction
Scripture: Isaiah 43:10; 44:5
You'll need a Bible and permanent markers or felt-tip pens.

Overview
After reading the words of Isaiah, we are reminded that if we truly belong to Christ, we should willingly and joyfully let everyone know about our relationship with him.

- This activity challenges worshippers' willingness to be publicly identified with God. It also creates opportunities to share Christ with others.

Read aloud Isaiah 43:10 and Isaiah 44:5. Say:

One of our tasks as Christians is to be witnesses for Christ and tell the

world who he is and what he has done. In the Old Testament, God speaks of those who would write his name on their hands. What a bold way to declare your allegiance to God. As we prepare to leave worship and take Christ's message into the world, I want to challenge you to identify yourself with Christ by writing his name on your hand. You are God's servants and have been chosen to boldly share his message with others.

Distribute markers, and give worshippers an opportunity to write something about God on their hands. You might suggest that they write the phrase "God reigns" or "Jesus lives." Challenge worshippers to leave the marks on their hands as long as possible throughout the coming week and to anticipate questions that might lead to discussions about Jesus.

(**Note:** Be sure and let worshippers know that the markers are permanent but will wear off within several days.)

No Barriers

Activity: Music experience
Scripture: Psalm 117; 1 Corinthians 12:12-13
You'll need a Bible and a songbook or hymnal printed in a language other than English.

Overview
Racism and nationalism are not part of God's plan for humanity. No group of people has exclusive rights to God's mercy and love; rather, God's intention is to draw all nations to himself.

• This activity provides a way to illustrate that God is a universal God and that we all have the opportunity to be brothers and sisters in Christ.

If a foreign language–speaking family belongs to your church, ask it to help with this worship activity. If not, arrange for a foreign language class from a local school to help. Ask the volunteers to attend worship and sing a carol or hymn to your congregation in a language other than English.

Before the music begins, read aloud Psalm 117 and 1 Corinthians 12:12-13. Say:

Isn't it wonderful that God understands every known language. God knows no barriers. No group has exclusive rights to God's mercy and love. His plan is to draw all nations to himself. As we listen to the following special music, let us reflect on all our Christian brothers and sisters across the world.

End with a prayer thanking God for the gift of salvation, which is available to all humankind.

First Love

Activity: Meditation
Scripture: 1 John 4:7-12; Revelation 2:3-4
You'll need a Bible, preprinted appreciation cards, pencils, and soft background music.

Overview
God gave us an example of eternal love when he sacrificed his Son. God loves us and desires our love in return.

• This activity helps worshippers focus on specific reasons why they love God and helps worshippers express their love in a memorable way.

Before the worship service, prepare a simple appreciation card for each participant. Use an 8 ½x11 piece of paper that's folded in half with the words "I love you because…" printed on the front. Place the cards on seats before worshippers arrive.

At an appropriate time in the service, read aloud 1 John 4:7-12 and Revelation 2:3-4. Say:

God wants to be our *first* love, to remain *first* in our hearts. When did you last tell God that you loved him? When I ask you that question in a few minutes, you won't have to search your memory because we're going to tell God right now.

Please pick up the cards you found on your seats and, for the next three minutes, write a love note to God. Why do you love him? What has he done for you? How do you feel about God? No one else will see

what you write. It's between you and God.

Have worshippers fill out the cards as soft music plays.

Afterward ask for a few volunteers to share part or all of what they wrote. Finally challenge worshippers to take home their notes and put them where they can see them each day. Let the notes be reminders not to take their loving relationships with God for granted.

From Above

Activity: Prayer, creative movement
Scripture: James 1:17

Overview
James reminds us that all the good blessings we receive are gifts from God.

• This activity helps participants recognize and thank God for the gifts they've received from him while recognizing God's desire for them to use the gifts to serve others.

When you're ready to begin, say:

> **As we begin this time of prayer, please stand with your hands stretched in front of you, palms up, and with your fists clenched.**

Pause until worshippers are in position.

Continue:

> **God gives good gifts to his children. Sometimes these gifts are nurturing relationships. Other times they are talents or opportunities. If you've ever received a good gift from God, open your right hand and continue to hold it, palm up, in front of you.**

> **God has used most of us at one time or another to share gifts with others. We teach Sunday school classes, lead Bible studies, offer listening ears to friends, take meals to those who are grieving, as well as perform a multitude of other ministries. If God has ever used you to serve another person, open your left hand and continue to hold it, palm up, in front of you.**

God uses his people to encourage and affirm each other in service to him. If you've ever received an encouraging word from someone or received help in a practical, caring way, hold the hand of another person near you.

Close with corporate prayer, thanking God for providing good gifts—and for using us to use our gifts to serve others.

Sing a New Song

Activity: Prayer, music experience
Scripture: Psalm 149:1-2
You'll need a Bible, sheets of paper, pens or pencils, soft music, and two volunteer readers.

Overview
The book of Psalms is really a songbook filled with lyrics David and other psalmists wrote and offered to God in worship.

• This activity provides an opportunity for worshippers to accept the biblical challenge to sing a new song to the Lord as they write psalms of thanksgiving.

Read aloud Psalm 149:1-2. Say:

> Today we are going to write our own psalms to offer as worship to our awesome God.

Distribute pieces of paper and pencils to worshippers, and ask them to take two or three minutes to complete the following sentence as music plays softly: "I see God's mighty majesty in..."

After sufficient time, collect the written psalms, and give them to two volunteer readers. As the background music continues, say:

> Lord, we see your mighty majesty in...

Have your volunteers finish the sentence each time by alternately reading what's written on the pieces of paper.

A Witness for the Generations

Activity: Prayer, building dedication
Scripture: Joshua 22:26-29
You'll need a Bible.

Overview

After God had helped the Israelites capture the Promised Land, Reuben, Gad, and Manasseh decided to build an altar. Instead of building it to offer sacrifices, they built it as a witness to future generations symbolizing their commitment to worship God.

• This dedication of the altar in your sanctuary will serve to remind your congregation of the powerful testimony that this central symbol of worship carries.

As you begin worship, ask the following questions:
  • **What does this altar represent?**
  • **What was the purpose of the altar in the Old Testament?**
  • **How is our altar today like an Old Testament altar?**

After the worshippers have had an opportunity to answer, read aloud Joshua 22:26-29.

To conclude, lead them in the following prayer:

> **Dear God, as we gather today in worship, we offer you praise and thanksgiving. You are a God of faithfulness, and we want you to see us as a faithful congregation. We dedicate this altar today as a symbol of our offerings and sacrifices of praise. May it stand as a witness to our heritage of praise and worship. May it stand as a witness to future generations so they will know that we praise the living God here. In Jesus' name, amen.**

Streams of Water

Activity: Benediction
Scripture: Psalm 42:1-2

You'll need a Bible, individual packets of saltines (like those supplied in restaurants), and small bottles of water.

Overview

Just as a deer depends on water to survive, we depend on God. Those who seek God will be satisfied.

• This activity provides a vivid illustration about what it means to hunger and thirst for righteousness.

Place the bottles of water near the church exit to be ready for worshippers immediately after the service ends.

Just before the benediction, have ushers distribute a packet of saltines to each worshipper. Instruct congregation members to eat the crackers as you read aloud Psalm 42:1-2.

Say:

> Think about a deer being hunted…stalked…knowing a wolf is closing in as she carefully picks her way across the rocks. She's climbing, her hooves slipping on the smooth stones. Her blood pounds in her ears as she picks her way up the rocky hillsides, seeking somewhere to hide. But she finds few trees and little brush in which to conceal herself. And behind her, growing ever closer, she hears the wolf crashing through the brush.
>
> Think about how her throat is parched; is it from fear or the sheer physical exertion of her flight for safety? There is no water here. She left the river far below. When she cranes her neck to look, she sees the river threading its way through the green valley below, tumbling and rolling, clear and fresh—cool. Between her and this life-giving refreshment is the wolf.
>
> She feels her throat ache. She's thirsty…so thirsty. She'd give anything to renew her strength with a long, refreshing drink of water, to feel the water splash on her body.
>
> Her lungs burn, and her heart almost explodes with the agony of climbing so high into the barren hills so far from the life-giving water below.
>
> Can you feel her thirst? "As the deer pants for streams of water, so my soul pants for you, O God."

As you leave worship today, the ushers will hand you a bottle of cool, refreshing water. As you prepare to go, commit yourself to seeking after God this week just as "the deer pants for streams of water."

Take Me Out to the Ball Game

Activity: Offering
Scripture: 2 Corinthians 9:7-8
You'll need a Bible and as many baseball caps as you have offering plates.

Overview

At one time or another during every baseball season, the emotions of a particular congregation are bound to run high. Perhaps your church softball team has won the tournament or the neighborhood Little League team is going to the finals. Maybe a big game conflicts with your service, but the faithful are at church.

• Since Paul suggests that we be cheerful givers, this activity calls for the use of baseball caps to collect the offering instead of your traditional offering plates.

Brief the ushers ahead of time about the use of baseball caps as offering plates so they won't be caught off-guard. Keep the caps hidden until it is time to use them.

When you are ready to begin the offering, read aloud 2 Corinthians 9:7-8. Then preface the collection with some comments about the event you know the congregation is thinking about. Challenge worshippers to smile as they give.

You might even suggest to your church organist or keyboard player that this would be a great time to strut his or her "Wrigley Field" stuff to add to the ambiance.

(**Variation:** If this works well for your congregation, try using football helmets on Super Bowl Sunday or fishing hats for Father's Day!)

Grow in Grace

Activity: Benediction

Scripture: 2 Peter 3:18

You'll need copies of the "Grow in Grace" responsive reading (p. 70).

Overview

Peter reminds us that as Christians, we always have room to grow. Finding ways to draw closer to Christ will prepare us to stand in times of trouble.

• This activity provides an opportunity for the congregation to read 2 Peter 3:18 together as a final charge and dismissal from the worship service.

Before the benediction, distribute copies of the responsive reading (p. 70). Lead worshippers in the responsive reading.

Praise the Lord

Activity: Call to worship

Scripture: Psalm 150

You'll need background music, an accompaniment track of the song "Make His Praise Glorious" by Sandi Patti, a soloist to sing the words along with the accompaniment track, a sound system, a photocopy of the "Praise the Lord: A Reading From Psalm 150" handout (p. 72) for all worshippers, and six volunteer readers.

Overview

Psalm 150 reminds us that all creation praises God everywhere and in many ways. The words encourage us to praise God every day.

• This activity provides worshippers with an opportunity to act on the challenge of Psalm 150 and praise God in a responsive reading (p. 72).

At the appropriate time, have the ushers distribute the responsive reading to worshippers, and have the readers prepare to begin the call to worship. They can either stand together at the front of the worship area or be dispersed throughout the congregation. Begin the background music, and have the readers lead the congregation

Grow in Grace

(2 Peter 3:18)

Leader: When you leave this place today, what are you to do?

Congregation: We are to grow in grace.

Leader: When you leave the worship area today, what are you to do?

Congregation: We are to grow in knowledge.

Leader: When you leave this place of worship today, whose grace and knowledge will you grow in?

Congregation: Our Lord and Savior Jesus Christ.

Leader: And the people of God said...

Congregation: "To him be glory both now and forever. Amen."

in the responsive reading.

When the reading is complete, have the soloist sing "Make His Praise Glorious."

Nehemiah and the Wall

Activity: Creative movement, call to worship
Scripture: Nehemiah 2:17-18
You'll need a Bible, at least one small box per family (shoe boxes work well), and markers. (**Note:** If feasible, you may want to have a box for every participant. You might also consider asking worshippers to bring boxes for themselves along with a few extras.)

Overview
It takes unity to accomplish any great task. When Nehemiah said to the people of Jerusalem, "Come, let us rebuild the wall," they began the work together.

• This activity provides an opportunity for the congregation to recognize the importance of working together to complete a task such as rebuilding the wall of Jerusalem.

Place two or three markers at the end of each row before the service.

As participants come into the worship area, have ushers distribute at least one box per family. When you're ready to begin this activity, read aloud Nehemiah 2:17-18. Say:

Spiritual renewal often begins with the vision of one person, as it did with Nehemiah. But great visions are usually accomplished through teamwork. Today we are going to use teamwork to build a replica of the wall as a reminder of the importance of working together as Christians.

Instruct worshippers to use the markers at the end of each row to write their family names on their individual boxes. When they're finished, call the families forward to begin stacking their boxes together. (**Note:** You might ask the ushers to help with the wall assembly.)

While the "wall" is being built, have the instrumentalists play a song.

When worshippers return to their seats, process the activity by asking:
• **What would have been the likely outcome of Nehemiah's construction**

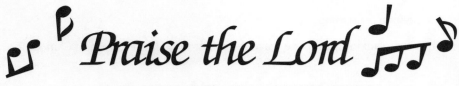

Praise the Lord

A Reading From Psalm 150

Reader 1: Praise God in his sanctuary; praise him in his mighty heavens. Let everything that has breath...

Congregation: Praise the Lord!

Reader 2: Praise him for his acts of power; praise him for his surpassing greatness. Let everything that has breath...

Congregation: Praise the Lord!

Reader 3: Praise him with the sounding of the trumpet, praise him with the harp and lyre. Let everything that has breath...

Congregation: Praise the Lord!

Reader 4: Praise him with tambourine and dancing, praise him with the strings and flute. Let everything that has breath...

Congregation: Praise the Lord!

Reader 5: Praise him with the clash of cymbals, praise him with resounding cymbals. Let everything that has breath...

Congregation: Praise the Lord!

Reader 6: Let everything that has breath...

Congregation: Praise the Lord!

project had the people not agreed to work together?

• What does Nehemiah's project, and our activity this morning, teach us about being the church together?

The Great Commission

Activity: Benediction, creative movement
Scripture: Matthew 28:19-20
You'll need a Bible and two volunteers.

Overview
According to the Gospel of Matthew, Jesus' final words were a charge to send his disciples out into the world to make more disciples. Jesus' great commission challenges us to do the same. From Jesus' commission we understand that we are to bring others to Christ as we go about our daily work and activities.

• As an appropriate end to worship, this activity provides an opportunity for the congregation to recognize the importance of being active in fulfilling the great commission.

Prior to the worship service, secure two people to help you with this activity. One of the volunteers will be representing a church that is experiencing little growth, while the other one will be representing a church that is showing dynamic growth.

Just prior to the end of worship, call your two helpers to the front. Place Leader 1 at the left of the worship area and Leader 2 at the right. Say:

These two people represent the leaders of two different congregations. They are going to go out into the congregation and bring people to the front with them in the symbolic act of building a church.

Leader 1 will continue to go out into the congregation and bring back one person at a time. Leader 2 will bring back a person, and then both of them will go out and each bring one additional person back. Then the four will each go out and bring in another person. The activity will continue until all the worshippers have come forward.

After all worshippers are assembled at the front, read aloud Jesus' great commission from Matthew 28:19-20. Then ask:

- **Which of the two groups is most like a New Testament church and why?**
- **How does participating in this activity challenge us as we leave worship today?**

End with a prayer, asking God for courage to carry out Christ's challenge to bring others to God.

We Shall Be Your Witnesses

Activity: Creative reading, call to worship, benediction

Scripture: Acts 1:8

You'll need a Bible and, for each participant, a photocopy of the "We Shall Be Your Witnesses" handout (p. 75).

Overview

Acts 1:8 reminds us that we, too, belong to Jesus' circle of witnesses and, by the power of the Holy Spirit, are challenged to spread the gospel.

- This activity provides an opportunity for the congregation to verbally acknowledge the importance of being a witness to the gospel and of leading others to Christ.

Either include copies of the handout in worship bulletins or have ushers distribute them at the appropriate time. Read aloud Acts 1:8, and say:

> **Scripture teaches us that when we become Christians and receive the power of the Holy Spirit, an important part of our mission becomes leading others to Christ by showing and telling what God has done for us. Let us acknowledge this charge as we join together in the responsive reading.**

WE SHALL BE YOUR WITNESSES

Leader: When you come together in this place, what shall you do?

Congregation: We shall be your witnesses!

Leader: When the Holy Spirit comes upon you, what shall you do?

Congregation: We shall be your witnesses!

Leader: When you go out into the city, what shall you do?

Congregation: We shall be your witnesses!

Leader: When you go out into the hillside, what shall you do?

Congregation: We shall be your witnesses!

Leader: When you go out into the world, what shall you do?

Congregation: We shall be your witnesses!

Banner Prayers

Activity: Prayer

Scripture: Matthew 7:7-11

You'll need a large cloth banner (a sheet or another piece of cloth), fabric markers, and a small table.

Overview

Jesus instructed us to present our requests to God and to trust that God will give good things to his children.

• This activity gives participants a creative way to bring their prayers before God.

Prior to worship, hang the banner in the main worship entrance. Place the markers on a table beside the banner. As people enter the worship area, have ushers invite them to write their prayer requests on the banner with the fabric markers. Be sure to have ushers let people know that they can be creative in presenting their prayer requests either through phrases or symbols.

At the appropriate time during the worship service, have two ushers bring the banner to the front of the worship area and lay it on the altar or hold it up where worshippers can see it.

Spend some time in prayer, bringing the "banner prayers" before God.

Meditate Upon the Glories

Activity: Meditation

Scripture: Psalm 77:12-15

Overview

The psalmist speaks about meditating on the works of God. The memories of God's miracles and faithfulness sustained the Israelites during many trials and tribulations. Psalm 77:12-15 challenges us to take time out of our busy schedules to meditate upon God's mighty deeds.

• This activity provides worshippers with an opportunity to reflect on the nature of God without the distractions of everyday life. This time of quiet meditation during worship may surprise and provide discomfort for a few worshippers.

Sometime during your worship service, especially at a point at which everyone knows and anticipates what's coming next, ask everyone to stop for a moment.

Say:

> In today's busy world, very few of us take the time to actually stop and listen to God. We may set aside time to pray, to attend worship services and Bible classes, and to study the Scriptures—and certainly, there's nothing wrong with these activities! But to sit quietly with no agenda other than to be still and contemplate God's mighty deeds, is often out of place in the lives of most people.
>
> We're going to take the next few minutes for quiet contemplation. This is not a time of prayer, but a time to meditate upon the glories of God and the gift of our relationship with him.

If desired, have worshippers use Psalm 77:12-15 as a passage upon which to meditate.

Allow three to five minutes for quiet meditation. This will be quite a long time for those who are not used to spending time in meditation.

Afterward consider asking a few worshippers to share their reactions to the experience.

Passing the Good News

Activity: Creative movement
Scripture: Matthew 28:19; Mark 16:15
You'll need a beach ball or inflated balloon.

Overview
Jesus' challenge to preach his gospel to all the world (Matthew 28:19; Mark 16:15) was a commission not only to his disciples, but to all Christians. This commission is as relevant to our lives as it was to those of the early disciples.

• This activity provides a graphic reminder that all Christians need to be involved in the spreading of the gospel to non-Christians.

Begin by asking everyone to think of your meeting place as a sort of biblical time line. Designate one corner of your worship area, such as the back left section, to represent the days of the early Christians. Then designate the opposite corner to represent a generation that is not yet born.

Hold up the beach ball or balloon, and explain that it represents Christ's promise of eternal life. Say:

> **The object is to pass the good news from the early Christians along all the other generations until it ends up with the future generation. Use as many people as possible to help pass the good news (or the ball) from one generation to the next.**

Toss the ball to the "early Christians," and let them begin passing it so that each person gets a chance to help move it along.

About three-quarters of the way through the process, halt the proceedings and say:

> **I'm sorry, but that's all the time we have; there are more important things to do now. Some of you will just have to go without the good news.**

Engage worshippers in a short discussion and reflection by asking:
- **How was waiting to have the ball passed to you like non-Christians waiting to hear the good news about Jesus?**
- **What are ways Christians today can make sure they don't "drop the ball" in spreading the news about Jesus?**

This Little Light

Activity: Music experience
Scripture: Matthew 5:14-16; Mark 4:21
You'll need a Bible, one candle per worshipper (like those used for Christmas Eve worship), matches, and a children's choir or group of volunteer children.

Overview
Jesus doesn't expect us to hide our faith like a lamp hidden under a bowl since a

hidden light would have no purpose. Jesus calls us to be the light of the world and to let our faith be evident to others.

• Through this activity, worshippers will be renewed in their faith by the timeless simplicity of children's praise. Don't let Christmas Eve be the only candlelight service your congregation enjoys. Combine the peacefulness of candlelight with the simple faith of the little children in your church for a touching act of praise that's as simple as it is powerful.

A week or two before this activity, ask your children's leader to have the young children in the church practice the well-known children's song "This Little Light of Mine." Let the kids know they'll be leading the "grown-up" church in singing the song.

As participants enter the worship area, give each one a handheld candle. When you are ready for this activity, read aloud Matthew 5:14-16. Then have the children enter the worship area.

(**Note:** If you feel it's safe and there is enough supervision, let the children hold lighted candles as they stand and face the congregation. If not, have children hold flashlights instead.)

Before the song, ask a few of the children to share something they know about Jesus. Afterward, have ushers help light the worshippers' candles. When the candles are all lit, dim the lights, and let the children sing through the song once.

Next ask the congregation members to hold their candles high as they join the kids in singing the song again.

Gathered in His Name

Activity: Prayer
Scripture: Matthew 18:20
You'll need a Bible.

Overview
Jesus' words in Matthew 18:20 remind us that whenever two or more believers are gathered in his name, and pray according to God's will, Jesus will be there with them.

• In this activity, the power of unified praying and sharing is emphasized.

Have worshippers form groups of three. Depending on the comfort level of your group, you may ask trios to hold hands for this activity. Read aloud Matthew 18:20, and let participants know that this time is for them to pray together. Reassure them that Jesus will be in their midst as they pray together.

This time of prayer can be used in many ways. You can use it when the church is facing a decision that requires concentrated prayer and guidance. Or you can use it when you have prayer concerns, such as illnesses, that you want to bring before the congregation. Or you may want to turn this prayer time into one of personal sharing by asking each person to bring a prayer concern before his or her group.

However it's used, this special time of prayer will foster a sense of intimacy both among partners and with Jesus.

Let the Children Come

Activity: Pre-service greeting
Scripture: Matthew 18:2-3; 19:14; 21:15-16

Overview

In the book of Matthew, Jesus uses a little child as the example of the kind of faith that opens the kingdom of heaven (18:2-3). Later Jesus welcomes little children into his midst, again explaining their place in his kingdom (19:14). And Jesus even points to children's praise (21:15-16) as acceptable and worthy.

• Use this activity as a smile-inspiring way to greet worshippers as they arrive for the service. It's especially effective when it's time to kick off your VBS or when you know you'll be welcoming newcomers.

A few weeks in advance, ask your director of children's education to work with you in setting up this simple activity. Have a preschool or early elementary class be the greeters before your worship service.

Explain to the children that their job will be to welcome everyone and assist worshippers to their seats for "grown-up" church. With very little prompting, these little children will set an example of simple faith and the happiness to serve that comes naturally to kids. In addition, the children's joy in simply being in church is sure to shine through.

The Beloved Psalm

Activity: Creative reading, prayer
Scripture: Psalm 23; James 5:16
You'll need same-translation Bibles.

Overview

The twenty-third Psalm has long been recognized as one of infinite comfort in reminding us of God's love, protection, and faithfulness. Combining its words of solace with James' exhortation to pray for others (5:16) can invoke a very real picture of the power and results of prayer.

• This simple rendition of a beloved psalm will provide the opportunity to lift a friend's name before the Lord.

At the desired point in your worship service, ask each person to think of someone they care about and would like to lift before God in prayer. After a few moments, lead the group in reading Psalm 23 aloud together in unison. Say:

> **As we read Psalm 23 in unison, instead of using the personal pronouns "me" and "I" throughout the reading, substitute the person's name you want to pray for. So instead of saying, "The Lord is my shepherd, I shall not be in want," you might be saying, "The Lord is Tiffany's shepherd, she shall not be in want"; another person may substitute the name David or Claire.**

As the entire group reads together, hearing the collection of names and recognizing the prayerful desires for those mentioned will be a simple yet powerful example of Christian faith in action.

Eagle's Wings

Activity: Prayer, creative movement, music experience

Scripture: Isaiah 40:28-31

You'll need the words to the chorus of the song "On Eagle's Wings" by Michael Joncas, 1979 (commonly available through various church musical publications), and photocopies of the "Movements for the Refrain of 'On Eagle's Wings'" handout (p. 83) inserted into bulletins.

Overview

Often our lives are filled with despair and hopelessness. Yet through the power of prayer and the reassurance of Scripture, we are assured that God is with us.

• This activity provides an opportunity to use physical movement to reinforce God's care for us. It can have very powerful effects on participants.

Prior to the worship service, make photocopies of the handout (p. 83) to be included as part of the bulletin. Consider asking a few people ahead of time to prepare to make prayer requests during the service.

Before the actual prayer time arrives, teach the chorus of the song "On Eagle's Wings" and the movements that go with it.

At the appropriate time, invite participants to verbally make their prayer requests. After each request, lead the congregation in singing the chorus and performing the movements as a way of praying for that person. Allow plenty of time for this prayer event.

(**Variation 1:** In a large congregation, praying for worshippers individually may not be an option; instead choose certain prayer needs such as "those suffering from illness," "those who want to grow closer to God," and so forth. Have all those who are in need of prayer pertaining to this particular request stand while the rest of the congregation sings the chorus to them.)

(**Variation 2:** Have everyone participating in this activity form a circle for the prayer time. When a worshipper makes a prayer request, that person can step into the circle, if physically able, while everyone sings the chorus to him or her. If verbally naming a specific prayer concern is difficult for some people, reassure them that they can simply stand in the circle without saying anything and receive the group's blessing.)

Movements for the Refrain of "On Eagle's Wings" by Michael Joncas

Movement for eagle's wings: Pull your arms back behind your body, bent at the elbows.

Movement for the breath of dawn: Move your arms from the previous position until they're outstretched in front of your body.

Movement for the sun: With your arms still outstretched, move slightly from left to right.

Movement for the palm of God's hand: Bring your hands together in front of your body at your waist, cupping one hand in the other.

Peace Blessing

Activity: Benediction, music experience

Scripture: Luke 2:29-31

You'll need the words to the chorus of the song "Go Now in Peace" by Natalie Sleeth (commonly available through various church musical publications).

Overview

Simeon rejoices in his worship experience, blesses the Christ child, and then is dismissed "in peace."

• This activity provides an opportunity for worshippers to be dismissed in God's peace and to pass the same blessing to another person.

If your congregation is unfamiliar with the chorus "Go Now in Peace," consider teaching it ahead of time.

When you are ready to end the worship service, say:

> **As we sing "Go Now in Peace," I will reach out and touch a person on the shoulder. That person should then touch another person, and everyone should continue in this manner so a "domino effect" occurs. Continue to keep your hands in place so that all worshippers are touching and being touched at once.**

Lead worshippers in singing "Go Now in Peace."

Salty Saints

Activity: Benediction

Scripture: Matthew 5:13-16

You'll need a Bible, small packets of salt (available in large quantities from wholesale grocery stores), and small baskets (optional).

Overview

In the sermon on the mount, Jesus challenged his followers with the importance of sharing the message of salvation with others. Jesus also anticipated our sometimes lackadaisical approach to the gospel by reminding us that our worth is in our "saltiness."

• This activity provides an object lesson which reminds us that as Christians we are the seasoning of love and light in the world and that we must not lose our savor.

Read aloud Matthew 5:13-16. Invite all worshippers who are able to come forward and each receive a packet of salt. For those unable to come forward, serve them or have ushers serve them. As you hand each person a packet of salt, say:

You are the salt of the earth; you are the light of the world.

For a large congregation, ushers or other volunteers can hand a basket of salt packets to the person at the beginning of each row. Then people can pass the baskets down the rows and say to each other, "You are the salt of the earth."

(**Variation:** Use this activity as part of a commissioning service by calling those to be commissioned forward and presenting them each with a salt packet and a charge.)

Bread of Life

Activity: Act of praise, celebration of the Lord's Supper
Scripture: John 6:48-51
You'll need a Bible, unsliced loaves of bread, and volunteers to serve bread.

Overview
The Gospel of John recounts Jesus' reference to himself as the "bread of life." By using that phrase, Jesus meant that those who accepted him would receive eternal life.

• This activity provides an opportunity for the congregation to thank God for giving them the Bread of Life.

Prior to worship, secure an adequate number of helpers to distribute the loaves of bread. At the appropriate time, call the volunteers forward, break off chunks of bread, and hand a chunk to each helper. As you hand the bread to each helper, say:

Jesus is the bread of life.

Have the helpers go into the congregation and begin passing the loaf, saying, "Jesus is the bread of life." As each person receives the loaf, he or she should break off a piece of bread and pass it on using the same words.

After all worshippers have received a piece of bread, read aloud John 6:48-51. Then have everyone eat the bread together and pray silently, praising God for the gift of his Son, Jesus Christ.

Sing to the Lord

Activity: Music experience

Scripture: Psalm 30:1-4

You'll need a Bible, copies of the hymn "I'll Fly Away," copies of the first verse of the hymn "Amazing Grace" (you can substitute other hymns or praise songs), and a guitar or other accompaniment (optional).

Overview

Psalm 30:1-4 reminds us that any time is appropriate to sing praises to God and celebrate our salvation.

• This activity provides a fun and meaningful way to sing and praise God. It is especially meaningful if you use hymns or songs that are well-known by worshippers.

Prior to worship, familiarize your accompanying musicians with this activity.

To set the mood for this music experience, read aloud Psalm 30:1-4. Then lead worshippers as they sing the first verse of "I'll Fly Away," immediately followed by the first verse of "Amazing Grace."

Go right back to the second verse of "I'll Fly Away," then immediately back to the first verse of "Amazing Grace."

Continue alternating *each* verse of the first hymn with the *first* verse only of the second well-known hymn or praise song.

Holidays

Christmas

Traditions

Activity: Call to worship, sharing time

Scripture: Luke 1:76

You'll need four families to share a Christmas tradition.

Overview

Prior to the ministry of Jesus, God sent John the Baptist to prepare the hearts of people to receive Christ. Christians celebrate the season of Advent to prepare their hearts for the coming of the Christ child at Christmas.

• This activity allows worshippers to hear how others have established traditions to keep the true meaning of Christmas. This activity takes place each Sunday for four weeks prior to Christmas Day.

Select one family for each Sunday throughout Advent who is willing to stand before the congregation and share a Christmas tradition unique to the family. The tradition should represent a significant way that family celebrates the holiness of Christ's birth during Christmas. It might include a special tradition on Christmas Eve or Christmas morning or any time throughout the season of Advent.

(**Variation:** You can combine this event with the lighting of Advent candles if your worship tradition uses them. After a family shares a Christmas tradition, have the family light the Advent candle for that Sunday. You might also consider using single members or retired couples or widows to share and light the Advent candles. This will give those members a sense of belonging and participation in what is often seen as a family holiday.)

Jesus Is Born

Activity: Call to worship, creative reading

Scripture: Luke 2:8-14

You'll need photocopies of the "Jesus Is Born!" handout (p. 90), folded and inserted into each bulletin or handed to each person at the beginning of the service.

Overview

As shepherds kept watch over their sheep in the dead of night, a choir of angels suddenly appeared and began proclaiming Jesus' birth and singing praises to God!

• This activity reminds participants to worship God for the majesty and wonder of Jesus' birth.

As the service is beginning, ask participants to refer to the "Jesus Is Born!" handouts. Lead the worshippers in the responsive call to worship. Be sure to read the "worship leader" part with plenty of expression and feeling to set the tone for the worship service to follow.

Your Scene

Activity: Meditation, prayer
Scripture: John 1:1-2; Philippians 2:5-8
You'll need a Bible.

Overview

Christ was with God in heaven from the beginning, but he gave up the glories of heaven to come to earth as a baby for the purpose of dying on the cross for us.

• In this activity, worshippers imagine giving up everything they have and relate that experience to what Christ gave up to be born on earth.

Ask worshippers to close their eyes and picture themselves in their favorite place in the world. Ask them to continue picturing the scene, adapting it with each new situation you present.

Say:

> **Now pretend that you're stripped of your job and your home.**

Pause.

> **Now you're stripped of your belongings—all of them, even your cars and clothes and food.**

Pause.

> **Now you're stripped of your friends; you have none.**

Pause.

Jesus Is Born!

(Luke 2:8-14)

Worship Leader: It was a night like any other. The shepherds sat in the darkness, watching over their sheep. The quiet darkness reminded them that the rest of the world was sleeping.

Congregation (in a whisper): Jesus is born.

Worship Leader: Suddenly an angel of the Lord appeared to the shepherds, and the glory of the Lord shone around them, and they were terrified. But the angel said to them, "Do not be afraid. I bring you good news of great joy that will be for all the people."

Congregation (loudly): Jesus is born!

Worship Leader: "Today in the town of David a Savior has been born to you; he is Christ the Lord."

Congregation: His name is Jesus!

Worship Leader: "This will be a sign to you: You will find a baby wrapped in cloths and lying in a manger."

Congregation: Jesus is born—God and human in one!

Worship Leader: Suddenly a great company of the heavenly host appeared with the angel, praising God and saying...

Congregation: "Glory to God in the highest, and on earth peace to men on whom his favor rests."

Worship Leader: Jesus has come to show us what God is like.

Congregation: Jesus has come to redeem us.

Worship Leader: Praise God! Jesus is born!

Now you're stripped of your family, and you're all alone.

Pause.

What does your scene look like?

Pause.

Now, finally, you're stripped of your life.

Pause.

What a horrible experience to imagine. We would never choose these things to happen to us or anyone we love. In fact, we would fight against it.

Read aloud Philippians 2:5-8.

Say:

Continue to keep your eyes closed. Now think about God's Son, the Christ, in heaven with his Father. Now think about Jesus as he gives up—willingly—his home in heaven, his power, his glory. And for what? To be born a human baby to a poor couple more than two thousand years ago in Bethlehem. He gave up everything not to live a lavish, royal life here on earth, but to die. Can you picture that? *That's* why we celebrate Christmas.

End with a corporate prayer.

Baby Powder and the Holy Child

Activity: Call to worship, meditation
Scripture: Luke 2:7
You'll need one-inch strips of fabric (old receiving blankets torn into strips work well), baby powder, and a box.

Overview
One of the truly riveting aspects of our faith is that the God of the universe chose to reveal himself in human form. The story of Christ's birth in the most humble of surroundings reawakens our conceptual struggle each holiday season as we renew our commitment to this holy God-child.

- This activity provides a sensory tool to help worshippers feel the meaning of Christmas as they experience the smell and touch of Christ's humanity while, at the same time, considering his deity.

Prior to worship place the strips of cloth into a box. Sprinkle baby powder over the strips just before worshippers arrive. As participants enter the worship area, ask them each to take one of the strips and hold it throughout the service.

As a call to worship, say:

Hold up your piece of fabric to your face and feel its softness.

Pause.

Now smell it. Think about the memories that its touch and smell bring to you.

Pause.

Turn to a partner and take a moment to share some of the memories that have come to mind.

After a few minutes, say:

It's amazing to think that God almighty came into the world as a tiny baby—weak, vulnerable, and dependent on a human mother and father. What would it have been like to feed baby Jesus? What would it have been like to rock Jesus to sleep in your arms? What would it have been like to watch Jesus as he slept?

I want to challenge you to hold this human image of Jesus in your minds and continue to feel and smell the fabric throughout worship. But at the same time, meditate upon the power, strength, and sovereignty of the risen Christ.

Encourage worshippers to keep the fabric strips after the service as bookmarks for the Christmas story in their Bibles.

Magi Trivia

Activity: Meditation, call to worship
Scripture: Matthew 2:1-12

You'll need candy canes or similar treats for worshippers and a list of trivia questions about the Magi (see suggested questions below).

Overview

Much of what we know about the birth of Christ and the coming of the Magi has more to do with what tradition and secular culture has taught us rather than the truths of Scripture.

• This activity provides a fun opportunity to share Scripture about the Magi's visit to Christ. It works best if done prior to Scripture reading.

Prior to worship, prepare several trivia questions from the Matthew text. Questions might include the following:

> • **How many Magi visited Jesus at his birth?** *(The Bible doesn't say how many.)*
> • **What is another term for Magi?** *(Wise men)*
> • **Who was king of Judea when Jesus was born?** *(Herod)*
> • **How did the Magi know of Jesus' birth?** *(Star)*
> • **What gifts did the Magi offer?** *(Gold, incense, and myrrh)*
> • **Bonus: What did the gifts represent?** *(Gold represented deity; incense represented purity; myrrh represented death.)*

When you are ready to use this activity, say:

> **Often what we know about the traditions of Christmas—especially the coming of the Magi after the birth of Christ—comes from tradition rather than from what the Bible tells us. We are going to have some fun this morning by playing Magi Trivia.**

Ask the questions you have prepared. Provide people who answer correctly with a candy cane or special treat. Then hand out treats to all the worshippers for taking part in the trivia game. Keep the pace upbeat and positive.

Following the activity by reading aloud Matthew 2:1-12.

Christ the Lord Is Risen

Activity: Call to worship
Scripture: Luke 24:1-8
You'll need a Bible, black plastic and tape or other window coverings for every window in the worship area, three bathrobes, packages wrapped in cloth, and three female volunteers.

Overview
The resurrection of Jesus was a spectacular demonstration of God's victory over death.

• This dramatic re-enactment of the first record of Jesus' resurrection will leave a strong impression on your congregation.

Prepare the worship area for this Easter service by turning out all the lights and, if possible, covering all the windows with black plastic, cardboard, or blinds. The object is to make the worship area as dark as possible. Start the worship service by having three women dressed in robes enter from the back of the worship area. The women should carry the wrapped packages and walk slowly with their heads down. Just as they reach the altar at the front of the church, have an offstage reader dramatically read aloud Luke 24:1-8.

After the reading, have ushers turn on all the lights and slowly drop the coverings from all the windows to imitate dawn. When the worship area is filled with light, have the women run back down the aisle shouting, "Jesus is alive!"

Move immediately into a dramatic Easter song such as "Christ the Lord Is Risen Today" or "He's Alive."

What Are You Discussing?

Activity: Call to worship, creative reading
Scripture: Luke 24:13-17
You'll need a sound system with two microphones, five male volunteers and three female volunteers, and eight photocopies of the "What Are You Discussing?"

handout (p. 96).

Overview

Jesus' question to the men on the road to Emmaus created a point of entry into their lives that he still uses today: genuine interest in our daily affairs and conflicts. In a sense, by asking, "What are you discussing?" Jesus was asking, "Are you listening to what the world is saying, or are you listening to me by faith?"

• This activity is a call to worship that uses the question Jesus asked the men on the road to Emmaus as the basis for a behind-the-scenes mini-drama.

Prior to the worship service, recruit eight volunteers to act as dramatic readers. Give each a photocopy of the "What Are You Discussing?" handout (p. 96).

Set up a sound system with two microphones offstage and out of sight. Use one microphone for the person playing the interviewer and another for each of the other seven characters. If you can make your sound system project through different speakers, have the interviewer's voice come from the left of the worship area and the other voices come from the right of the worship area.

Have the readers stand offstage and perform the creative reading. When you are ready to begin this activity, provide worshippers with an introduction by saying:

> Jesus' question to the men on the road to Emmaus created a point of entry into their lives that he still uses today: genuine interest in our daily affairs and conflicts. In a sense, by asking, "What are you discussing?" Jesus was asking, "Are you listening to what the world is saying, or are you listening to me by faith?"

Who Shared With You?

Activity: Sharing time, offering
Scripture: Matthew 28:10; Mark 16:7; Luke 24:9-10; John 20:17; Romans 10:17
You'll need paper and pencils.

Overview

Each of the Gospel accounts of Easter includes, as one of the first reactions to the news of Jesus' resurrection, the injunction to go and tell someone else the glad tidings. This injunction is still important today, since as Christians we are still called to share the message of Jesus (Romans 10:17).

What Are You Discussing?

Interviewer: What are you discussing as you walk along?

Joanna: Mary! Did you really see him? All we knew was that his body was gone! But you really saw him? Do you think it was his ghost?

Mary: No, Joanna, it was really him. He wouldn't allow me to touch him because he hadn't returned to the Father yet, but he called out my name, and I knew. *I knew!* Only Jesus could have such depth in a single breath. It was him, Joanna. I have no doubt. He is risen.

(Pause for a few moments.)

Interviewer: What are you discussing as you walk along?

Simon Peter: *(Out of breath)* John! Is he in there? Where...what is this? These are the strips he was wrapped in. And the burial cloth. John! Get in here! John, what do you make of this?

(Pause for a few moments.)

Interviewer: What are you discussing as you walk along?

First Man: Where have you been? Haven't you heard about Jesus?

Second Man: He was crucified three days ago. Now we can't find his body. Our women say they have seen a vision of angels who said he is alive. The whole thing is crazy.

(Pause for a few moments.)

Interviewer: What are you discussing as you walk along?

Modern Woman: The whole thing is crazy. I thought we had a good life. At least it *seemed* good. Then I received this insane phone call. He won't even talk to me face to face. He doesn't want me to be here when he comes to get his things.

(Pause for a few moments.)

Interviewer: What are you discussing as you walk along?

Modern Man: Who does that guy think he is anyway? He has no right to sit in judgment of me! Maybe he'd better check out the plank in his own eye before he starts trying to preach about the speck in my eye!

Interviewer: "And beginning with Moses and all the Prophets, he explained to them what was said in all the Scriptures concerning himself" (Luke 24:27). *(Pause for dramatic effect.)* What are *you* discussing as you walk along? *(Pause again.)* What are *you* discussing as you walk along?

- This activity provides worshippers a time to reflect on the Christians who led them to faith in Jesus and challenges them to share the good news of Christ's resurrection with others. You can use this activity during the close of the Easter service, but it works equally well as a reflective activity on Good Friday. It can be as long or as short as you deem appropriate and can be done in pairs, small groups, or with the congregation as a whole.

Begin by asking worshippers to think about when they first heard about Jesus. Who told them about him? How old were they? What was the setting like? Have worshippers form small groups and share their experiences in as much detail as time allows, or simply ask each person to reflect silently.

Next ask worshippers to consider how their lives might be different if the people who told them about Jesus had remained silent. Again let everyone share or reflect in silence.

Have ushers distribute paper and pencils, and instruct each person to tear his or her paper in half. On one piece of paper, have each participant write a short thank you note to the person who first told him or her about Jesus. As the offering plates are passed, have worshippers place their thank you notes in the plates with their offerings as prayers of thanksgiving for those who shared their faith.

Next ask worshippers to think of people with whom they can share the news of Jesus' resurrection. Have them each write that person's name on the other sheet of paper. Encourage worshippers each to take these second pieces of paper home to remind and challenge them to tell that person about Jesus.

End by closing in prayer, either by leading it yourself or by asking worshippers to pray for each other in their groups.

Reflecting!
Remembering! Celebrating!

Activity: Meditation
Scripture: Matthew 27:27-61
You'll need a Bible.

Overview
God is good to those who hope in him and who quietly wait for salvation.

- This all-church Easter eve meditation (or optional camp-out) will give the members of your church an opportunity to spend time together. By creating an atmosphere of solemn meditation in the late evening, you'll be able to prepare for a joyous celebration on Easter morning.

Have worshippers meet together at an outdoors site for an evening gathering and meditation. Spend Saturday evening reflecting with the members of your church. As the night draws to a close, read about the crucifixion of Christ (Matthew 27:27-61) to your congregation. Afterward encourage participants to think about what Christ endured on the cross and return silently to their homes.

(**Variation:** Before Easter Sunday, reserve a campground large enough to accommodate your participants. Have them gather for a Saturday evening meditation as described above. Before the sun rises, gather worshippers and conduct an informal Easter worship service. Rather than concentrating on Christ's death, celebrate his resurrection and victory. **Note:** Consider planning the camp-out close enough to home so that following the sunrise service, families can return home and attend the regular Easter morning worship service.)

Father's Day

Fishers of Men and Children

Activity: Creative reading
Scripture: Deuteronomy 1:31b; Matthew 4:18-20
You'll need a fishhook taped to a wallet-size card for each father and photocopies of the "Father's Promise" handout (p. 99).

Overview
In Deuteronomy 1:31b, God illustrates his love and compassion for his people by using the example of a loving father.

• This activity reminds fathers that they are living examples of God's love in their children's lives and that responding to Jesus' challenge to be fishers of men includes leading their children to Christ.

Distribute photocopies of the "Father's Promise" handout (p. 99) by either inserting them into each bulletin or by handing them to all the fathers present in worship.

Father's Promise

Fathers say in unison:

I have been called to the highest position God gives to any man.

I am the leader of the most important institution in human history—the family.

I am provider, protector, model, and teacher—no matter how old my children are.

I am the earthly example of how the eternal Father loves his children.

My call to be a "fisher of men" challenges me to lead my children into a real and meaningful relationship with Christ.

I will continue to be responsive to my responsibilities as a loving Christian father.

Near the beginning of the service, ask the fathers to stand. Then lead them in reading the "Father's Promise" aloud and in unison. Afterward have the ushers distribute a card with an attached fishhook to each father. Encourage the men to keep these fishhooks in their wallets as reminders of the promise they read and of their critical roles in their children's relationships with God.

Remembering Fathers

Activity: Sharing time

Scripture: John 1:1-9

You'll need Bibles, a photocopy of the triangle handout (p. 101) for each worshipper, and pencils (optional).

Overview

An important part of John the Baptist's ministry was to point the way to Jesus. By his efforts, John prepared people to recognize and follow Jesus. In a similar manner, God gives us fathers or father figures that help us prepare for a strong relationship with Christ.

• This activity provides an opportunity for adults to share with one another about what their fathers, or other male role models, have taught them about following Jesus.

Give each worshipper a copy of the triangle handout.

Say:

> **Examine the three points of this triangle. Take a moment to think about how your father or grandfather has pointed you to Jesus. If you don't have a Christian father who has been active in your life, think about another significant father figure. Another male role model might include a Sunday school teacher, a coach, or a caring male friend who has played an important role in your life.**

After two to three minutes, invite the worshippers to form groups of four or five. Instruct the participants to choose one of the sides of the triangle and complete the sentence by sharing their thoughts with the others in the group.

Afterward take a few minutes to ask a few volunteers to share their reflections with everyone.

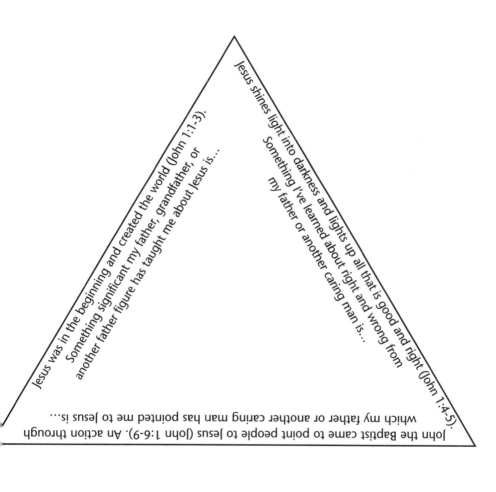

Jesus shines light into darkness and lights up all that is good and right (John 1:4-5).
Something I've learned about right and wrong from my father or another caring man is...

Jesus was in the beginning and created the world (John 1:1-3).
Something significant my father, grandfather, or another father figure has taught me about Jesus is...

John the Baptist came to point people to Jesus (John 1:6-9). An action through which my father or another caring man has pointed me to Jesus is...

Mother's Day

Honoring Mom

Activity: Sharing time

Scripture: Matthew 15:4

You'll need stationery and pens or pencils.

Overview

In the Gospel of Matthew, Jesus reminds us of the command to "honor your father and mother." Unfortunately, the skill of honoring one's father and mother has become somewhat nebulous in the modern world.

• This activity allows worshippers to model the attitude of honor as they celebrate Mother's Day.

Have worshippers make a special invitation to their mothers or mother figures to attend the worship service on Mother's Day. Either select participants ahead of time or ask for spontaneous volunteers to invite their mothers to the front of the worship area. With their mothers standing next to them, have the volunteers publicly complete the following statements:

• When I was a child, you taught me…
• When I became a teen, you taught me…
• Now that I am an adult, you are teaching me…

Invite those participants who don't have mothers present in worship to write a letter to their mothers and share the letters during worship.

Afterward encourage worshippers to honor their mothers in similar conversations or letters during the week ahead.

A Woman Is to Be Praised

Activity: Sharing time

Scripture: Proverbs 31:30b-31

You'll need a Bible; a small table decorated with a quilt, crocheted doily, hat box, antique brooch, and old photos of women; an empty basket; pencils; and blank pieces of paper or index cards inserted into bulletins or handed out at the appropriate time.

Overview

The writer of Proverbs knows that "a woman who fears the Lord is to be praised." This is an opportunity for that praise.

• This activity provides an opportunity to honor women without creating awkwardness for those who are childless. It can be done at any point during the worship service.

Prior to worship, place the table in a central location in the worship area, and decorate it.

When you are ready to begin the activity, invite worshippers each to think of and reflect upon a special woman who has made a difference in their lives such as a mother, teacher, or friend. When they have thought of someone, have them write on their pieces of paper the name of the person and why she is special. Invite two or three people to share a special story about a special woman in their lives.

Afterward read aloud Proverbs 31:30b-31. Invite everyone, in an act of praise for their mothers or other special women, to come forward and place their pieces of paper in the basket. Be sure to assist anyone who is unable to come forward.

After all the papers are in the basket, share the following prayer:

Eternal God, we praise you for each woman remembered here today. We thank you for the gift of mothers and for their nurturing that has touched our lives. We praise you for memories so fondly cherished. As we honor the gifts of women, may we celebrate your nurturing and love in our midst. Amen.

Palm Sunday

Missing the Messiah

Activity: Meditation
Scripture: Matthew 18:20; 21:1-11
You'll need a Bible and a chair decorated with a purple or royal red robe, a length

of red carpet in front of the chair, flowers around the chair, and a simple crown (if available).

Overview

The Jewish people waited thousands of years for their Messiah to arrive. They had opportunities to hear John the Baptist identify Jesus as the Messiah and to witness Jesus perform many miracles. Yet even when he rode into Jerusalem, they didn't recognize him. Jesus' appearance didn't match their expectations. They were blinded by their expectations so they missed the Messiah.

• This activity helps participants understand that just as the people in Jesus' day, many people today fail to recognize the Messiah in their midst. The activity also gives people an opportunity to consider how Jesus is present in their lives.

Before people arrive, decorate a chair in the front of the worship area so it looks like a throne. For decorations, use a length of red carpet, flowers, a crown, and anything tasteful and regal. If possible, arrange for a spotlight to shine on the throne.

When you are ready to begin, call the worshippers' attention to the throne.

Say:

> **There are several parallels between the Jewish people of Jesus' day and Christians today. Even after the Jews had witnessed Jesus' many miracles, when he rode into Jerusalem on what we traditionally celebrate as Palm Sunday, they didn't recognize him. Like many people in Jesus' day, the Savior doesn't always meet the expectations we have for him either. As a result, we often fail to recognize his presence in our midst. We're blinded by our expectations. So we miss him too. However, Jesus promises to be in our midst.**

Ask:

> **What are some ways Jesus is present in our midst today?**

Read aloud Matthew 18:20, and point again to the throne on stage. Explain that Jesus' triumphal entry didn't just happen thousands of years ago. It's happening now in the hearts and lives of his followers.

Transition quickly to praise and worship songs that address God directly. Follow the songs with a time of prayer, with people standing and praising God.

The Rocks Will Cry Out

Activity: Call to worship, creative movement

Scripture: Luke 19:28-40

You'll need a Bible; wide rubber bands; and enough flat, hand-size river rocks that are approximately two to three inches in diameter for each child to have two.

Overview

On what we celebrate as Palm Sunday, Jesus reminded those who would have rebuked the crowd that if men were to keep silent, the stones would cry out.

- This activity requires the help of your children's department to assist in a unique "rock band" to process into the worship area and accompany your worship music.

Prior to the worship service, enlist the help of your children's department to assist in a unique rock band. You'll need to allow time for practice. Provide each child with two rocks, and help children place rubber bands around their hands to help hold the rocks in their palms. Demonstrate how they can stabilize the rocks with their thumbs and hit the rocks together to make a clicking sound. Let the children practice the processional songs they will accompany using the rocks as percussion instruments.

On Palm Sunday, have your instrumentalists play traditional processional music as the children parade into the worship area, keeping time to the music with their rocks. When the children reach their designated area, have a reader read aloud Luke 19:28-40, concluding the reading by saying:

> **Hear the words of the Lord, and be reminded to praise the Lord joyfully in the presence of these unique instruments.**

Pentecost

Experience the Wind

Activity: Benediction

Scripture: Acts 2:2

You'll need a large, powerful fan and an extension cord.

Overview

God made his presence known in a spectacular way on Pentecost. The sound of a violent wind pointed to the power of the Holy Spirit for the first Christian converts.

• The sensation of hearing and feeling wind during this activity helps worshippers get a glimpse of the impact of the Spirit's presence on Pentecost.

Place a fan at the front of your worship area. The larger and noisier the fan, the better. Prior to the benediction, turn on the fan to high. Then invite participants to walk in front of the fan and gather at the front of the worship area. After they have gathered, and as they continue to listen to the sound of the rushing wind, invite worshippers to spend two or three minutes in a time of silent prayer and renewal.

Afterward close worship by praying for a powerful movement of the Holy Spirit in the lives of your worshippers.

(**Variation:** Consider setting out the fan and letting it blow throughout the worship service as a constant reminder of the Holy Spirit's presence.)

Among All Generations

Activity: Call to worship
Scripture: Acts 2:5-6
You'll need a Bible and some helpers including a preschooler, another child, a teenager, a young adult, a middle-aged adult, and a senior adult.

Overview

During the first Pentecost following Jesus' resurrection, people of all nationalities heard the Holy Spirit speak in their own language. Today God still transcends all barriers to bring unity and understanding.

• This call to worship illustrates that God's Holy Spirit continues to speak to all generations of Christians.

A few days prior to worship, enlist the help of the volunteers listed above. Each will be invited during worship to give a sixty-second testimony about how God helps him or her to live each day.

Use the following examples to provide the helpers ideas of what they might share:
    • The preschooler might sing "Jesus Loves Me."

- The other child could talk about how Jesus helps him or her play fairly.
- The teenager could speak about how Jesus keeps him or her focused on school in the midst of other pressures.
- The adult might speak about Jesus' help in the workplace or about parenting.
- The senior adult could define what wisdom is and how to use it.

At the appropriate time, call the helpers forward. Begin with the youngest, and move to the oldest. After each person has spoken, read aloud Acts 2:5-6. Say:

Each of these Christians has shared from his or her own experience with God's Holy Spirit. Regardless of age or experience, if we take time to listen, we can hear God's truth from one another. God's Spirit speaks in many languages and in each of our hearts just as he did on the first Pentecost following Jesus' death and resurrection.

Thanksgiving

The Lord Has Been Good

Activity: Sharing time, prayer
Scripture: Psalm 13:6; Ephesians 5:20; Philippians 4:6

Overview
Paul reminds us that an important part of our Christian faith is in *"giving thanks…for everything* (Ephesians 5:20) and then challenges us to make thanksgiving the foundation upon which our hopes and prayers are built (Philippians 4:6).

- This activity provides worshippers an opportunity to share why they are thankful to be part of the church family.

At the appropriate time during worship, remind everyone about the importance of giving thanks, especially so near the holiday in which we celebrate all for which we have to be thankful.

Ask worshippers each to take approximately five minutes to share with two or three other people near them one reason they are thankful to be part of the church family. Prompt worshippers by suggesting that they remember times they were touched by something or someone within the congregation.

(**Note:** Keep in mind that visitors may be present in worship. Invite them each to share with two or three people where they are from and what about their own lives they're thankful for.)

Afterward ask a few volunteers to share with everyone their reasons for being thankful. End with a prayer to offer thanks to God for so many wonderful blessings.

(**Variation:** A lower-risk alternative is to contact a few members ahead of time and ask them to be prepared to take a moment when called upon to stand and share why they are thankful to be part of the church family.)

Come Before Him

Activity: Benediction
Scripture: Psalm 95:1-2
You'll need index cards; pens or pencils; and copies of the hymn "Come Ye Thankful People" or the chorus "Give Thanks" (both available in many hymnals).

Overview
Psalm 95:1-2 reminds us that God is worthy of joyful praise and therefore calls us to sing praises to the Lord.

• The familiar traditional melody of "Come Ye Thankful People" provides a choral benediction for your congregation to fulfill the words of Psalm 95:2: "Let us come before him with thanksgiving and extol him with music and song."

As worshippers enter the church, give each an index card and a pencil. Ask participants to write something they are thankful for. Ask for the cards to be returned in the offering plates. Have an usher return the cards to you before the end of the service.

For your benediction or closing prayer, randomly read some of the cards. Pause to allow the congregation to respond to each "thanks offering" by singing the first line of "Come Ye Thankful People." After you have read several cards, close the prayer by singing a full verse of the hymn.

(**Note:** If your congregation is not familiar with this hymn, consider using the chorus "Give Thanks" or another song of thanksgiving.)

Index

Worship Activity Index

Scripture Index